Sex in the Bible

Recent Titles in
Psychology, Religion, and Spirituality
J. Harold Ellens. Series Editor

Married to an Opposite: Making Personality Differences Work for You
Ron Shackelford

Sin against the Innocents: Sexual Abuse by Priests and the Role of the Catholic Church
Thomas G. Plante, editor

Seeing the Compassionate Life: The Moral Crisis for Psychotherapy and Society
Carl Goldberg and Virginia Crespo

Psychology and the Bible: A New Way to Read the Scriptures, 4 Volumes
J. Harold Ellens and Wayne E. Rollins, editors

SEX IN THE BIBLE

A New Consideration

J. Harold Ellens

Foreword by Donald Capps
Preface by Wayne G. Rollins

Psychology, Religion, and Spirituality

Westport, Connecticut
London

Library of Congress Cataloging-in-Publication Data

Ellens, J. Harold, 1932–
    Sex in the Bible : a new consideration / by J. Harold Ellens.
        p. cm.—(Psychology, Religion, and Spirituality, ISSN 1546–8070)
    Includes bibliographical references and index.
    ISBN 0–275–98767–1
    1. Sex—Biblical teaching. I. Title.
BS680.S5E45 2006
220.8'3067—dc22   2005036341

British Library Cataloguing in Publication Data is available.

Library of Congress Catalog Card Number: 2005036341
ISBN: 0–275–98767–1
ISSN: 1546–8070

First published in 2006

Praeger Publishers, 88 Post Road West, Westport, CT 06881
An imprint of Greenwood Publishing Group, Inc.
www.praeger.com

Printed in the United States of America

The paper used in this book complies with the
Permanent Paper Standard issued by the National
Information Standards Organization (Z39.48–1984).

10   9   8   7   6   5   4   3   2   1

To my four daughters: Deborah, the erudite Hebrew Bible scholar and teacher; Jacqueline, the creative artist and entrepreneur; Rebecca, the psycho-spiritual therapist and teacher; and Brenda, the ingenious veterinarian and surgeon. They are gifts to me of grace, and all of them are filled with it, having inherited the nature and spirit of my mother, Grace Kortman Ellens (1904–1994).

CONTENTS

SERIES FOREWORD

The interface between psychology, religion, and spirituality has been of great interest to scholars for a century. In the last three decades a broad popular appetite has developed for books that make practical sense out of the sophisticated research on these three subjects. Freud expressed an essentially deconstructive perspective on this matter and indicated that he saw the relationship between human psychology and religion to be a destructive interaction. Jung, on the other hand, was quite sure that these three aspects of the human spirit, psychology, religion, and spirituality, were constructively and inextricably linked.

Anton Boisen and Seward Hiltner derived much insight from both Freud and Jung, as well as from Adler and Reik, while pressing the matter forward with gratifying skill and illumination. Boisen and Hiltner fashioned a framework within which the quest for a sound and sensible definition of the interface of psychology, religion, and spirituality might best be described or expressed.[1] We are in their debt.

This series of general interest books, so wisely urged by Praeger, and particularly by its editors, Suzanne I. Staszak-Silva and Deborah Carvalko, intends to define the terms and explore the interface of psychology, religion, and spirituality at the operational level of daily human experience. Each volume of the series identifies, analyzes, describes, and evaluates the full range of issues, of both popular and professional interest, that deal with the psychological factors at play (1) in the way religion takes shape and is expressed, (2) in the way spirituality functions within human persons and shapes both religious formation and expression, and (3) in the ways that spirituality is shaped and expressed by religion. The interest is psycho-spiritual. In terms of the rubrics of the disciplines and the science of psychology and spirituality, this series of volumes investigates the operational dynamics of religion and spirituality.

The verbs "shape" and "express" in the above paragraph refer to the forces that prompt and form religion in persons and communities, as well as to the manifestations of religious behavior (1) in personal forms of spirituality, (2) in acts of spiritually motivated care for society, and (3) in ritual behaviors such as liturgies of worship. In these various aspects of human function, the psychological and/or spiritual drivers are identified, isolated, and described in terms of the way in which they unconsciously and consciously operate in religion, thought, and behavior.

The books in this series are written for the general reader, the local library, and the undergraduate university student. They are also of significant interest to the informed professional, particularly in fields corollary to his or her primary interest. The volumes in this series have great value for clinical settings and treatment models, as well.

This series editor has spent an entire professional lifetime focused specifically upon research into the interface of psychology in religion and spirituality. These matters are of the highest urgency in human affairs today when religious motivation seems to be playing an increasing role, constructively and destructively, in the arena of social ethics, national politics, and world affairs. It is imperative that we find out immediately what the psychopathological factors are that shape a religion that can launch deadly assaults upon the World Trade Center in New York and murder 3,500 people, or a religion that motivates suicide bombers to kill themselves and murder dozens of their neighbors weekly, and a religion that prompts such unjust national policies as preemptive defense; all of which are wreaking havoc upon the social fabric, the democratic processes, the domestic tranquility, the economic stability and productivity, and the legitimate right to freedom from fear, in every nation in the world today.

This present volume, *Sex in the Bible,* is an urgent and timely work, the motivation for which is surely endorsed enthusiastically by the entire world today, as we increasingly witness the progressive unfolding of the horrors of sexual abuse of women and children and other forms of sexual aberration in all societies on this planet, particularly in religious communities. What is going on in these cases? How are we to understand, stop, and heal this lethal epidemic? This volume proposes some answers, but most importantly this volume clarifies more specifically what the crucial questions are rather than setting forth all the answers.

Of course, not all of the influences of religion now or throughout history have been negative. Indeed, most of the impact of the great religions upon human life and culture has been profoundly redemptive and generative of great good. It is just as urgent, therefore, that we discover and understand better what the psychological and spiritual forces are that empower people of faith and genuine spirituality to give themselves to all the creative and constructive enterprises which, throughout the centuries, have made of human life the humane, ordered, prosperous, and aesthetic experience it can be at its best. Surely the forces for good in both psychology and spirituality far exceed the powers and proclivities toward the evil that we see so prominently in our world today.

This series of Praeger volumes is dedicated to the greater understanding of *Psychology, Religion and Spirituality,* and thus to the profound understanding and empowerment of those psycho-spiritual drivers that can help us transcend the malignancy of our pilgrimage and enormously enhance the humaneness and majesty of the human spirit, indeed, the potential for magnificence in human life.

J. Harold Ellens
Series Editor

FOREWORD

Book covers and dust jackets frequently include endorsements by individuals who have read an advance copy of a volume. Often an endorsement will say to potential purchasers of the book that if they are able to read only one book on the subject with which the book is concerned, this is the book they should read. I was asked to write this foreword before I had received an advance copy of J. Harold Ellens's *Sex in the Bible*. When I got it and finished reading it, my first thought was, "If you are able to read only one book on the subject of sex in the Bible, be sure to read this one!" My second thought was, "If you are able to read only two books on the subject of sex in the Bible, reread this book!" My third thought was, "If you have never read a book on the subject of sex in the Bible, read this book, and you will not need to read another one on this subject." My third thought probably went a bit too far, as it may seem to discourage readers from continuing to explore this endlessly fascinating subject, but my first two thoughts were right on target.

One reason that they were right on target is that this book is true to its title. It deals with all of the references to sex in the Bible. It does not simply pick and choose. The fact that it does not merely pick and choose testifies to the scholarly expertise, range, and experience of the author. Most biblical scholars become experts on one or two books of the Bible, or one or two biblical genres, or they specialize in either the Old or the New Testament and have a limited knowledge of the other one. These scholars often take a disdainful or amused view of pastors who necessarily preach on the whole

Bible, and they often view these pastors' sermons as evidence of the bad things that can happen when a preacher's biblical knowledge is a mile wide and an inch deep. J. Harold Ellens is a biblical scholar whose knowledge is both deep and wide, and he is also a pastor whose pastoral sensitivities and judgments are deeply rooted in his knowledge of biblical texts.

He is more, though, than an accomplished biblical scholar and pastor. He is also a trained clinical psychologist with years of practical experience as a therapist. This training and experience affords a rare sensitivity to the healthy and unhealthy features and effects of biblical texts. It also enables him to draw on his knowledge of clinical research on the nature of human sexuality, as when he reports on studies of the chemistry of sexual passion or notes the relationship between sexual misbehaviors and borderline personality disorders.

Impressive as these professional credentials are, they would not count for much if he were not also a person of great humanity and generosity of spirit. This humanity and spirit may well have their origins in good parenting, and their strengthening in good marital relations, but the reader of this book will find inescapable the fact that such humanity and spirit is also a tribute to the formative influence of the Bible itself. J. Harold Ellens is able to write so well about the Bible because he is a product of it. When he makes a broad or general observation about the biblical way of thinking—its overall perspective—I trust this observation because I know that he is not only biblically informed but also biblically formed. He is as much a biblical man as the men who are talked about in the Bible, even more so, in fact, because they did not have the advantage of the experience of being avid readers of the Bible itself, a book that, in his own words, has "an endless fascination for us."

But enough about the author. Interesting as he is in his own right, his topic is what draws the reader, like a moth to the flame, to the book that he has written. And precisely here a personal confession is warranted. I am not a person who would normally pick up a book on sex and the Bible and think that I am in for absorbing reading. This expectation is probably due to my inherent suspicion that a book on sex and the Bible will make sex seem as dull as dishwater. This suspicion, however, is precisely what the book seeks to challenge. If you think the Bible has a jaundiced or puritanical view of sex, this book will make you think otherwise. If you do not believe me, I would invite you to place a bookmark here and immediately flip forward to chapter five, where you will be treated to a delightful, indeed arousing, account of the sexual romp in the hay depicted in Song of Songs. Sex does not get any better than this.

But like the eighteenth century midwives' manual that titillated the teenage boys in the Massachusetts town where Jonathan Edwards was the principal pastor, this book is also enlightening. There is so much to be learned from this relatively small book that I can only highlight what were for me the most important new learnings.

One such learning is that the Bible generally assumed a social context in which polygamous marriage was the norm. As Ellens explains, this practice had various social benefits, including the protection of women from poverty and prostitution. On the other hand, this practice had several negative side effects, particularly the fact that wives were jealous of one another because they suspected spousal favoritism or envied the fecundity of their husband's other wives. Nonetheless, this social institution of polygamy reveals a deeper truth about the biblical understanding of sexuality, namely, that there was a concern to create a workable social order, one in which the individual members of the society were not subject to extreme poverty, abjection, and abuse. It was not a perfect system by any means, but the very fact that consideration was given to the problems that would otherwise arise if this societal norm were not in place may well come as a surprise to those of us who believe that enlightened views on sexuality originated with us.

Another such learning is that biblical references to homosexual acts will be completely misunderstood by us if we do not take two very important contextual factors into account. One is the central importance in ancient Near Eastern societies of the fundamental rule of hospitality to strangers, a rule that meant that anyone who is temporarily an occupant of a person's residence is assured of safety and protection. Thus, the story of Genesis 19:1–29 about the citizens who tried to break into Lot's house in order to violate the men who were his guests is not a story about homosexual desire, primarily, but about the fundamental importance of the rule of hospitality. As Ellens concludes after a thorough exegetical analysis and hermeneutical interpretation of this story:

> Quite plainly, the proscription voiced by the passage, through the judgment Lot pronounces upon and against the citizens [who seek entry into his home], is viewed by Lot himself as a proscription against a breach of the hospitality laws. Though the verb, *know,* clearly implies sexual behavior, and in this case, apparently, abusive homosexual intent on the part of the mob, Lot seems not to care at all about that side of things in the story, neither does the story express any concern or judgment about whether or what kind of sexual behavior is intended. The implied sexual behavior seems not to be the issue at stake here. What is at stake is the inviolable

prescription for hospitality to strangers in the social and legal code of the ancient Near East.

The second important contextual factor is that specific biblical pro-scriptions of homosexual acts had to do with the fact that these were among the ritual practices that were common in pagan worship. These ritual practices—which included fornication with animals and even child sacrifice—were prohibited in the public worship of the God of Israel because they were considered idolatrous, an "abomination" in the temple of God. In Paul's letter to the Romans, these prohibitions were understood to be applicable to Christian worship as well. As Ellens explains, however, these proscriptions against homosexual acts in the context of worship have no relevance to homosexual behaviors outside the context of worship. Het-erosexual fornication in worship services would be no less an abomination to the God of Israel and the God of early Christianity.

A third important learning concerned the relationship between what Ellens calls "a small" and "completely irrelevant story these days" and the opposition of the Roman Catholic Church to one of the major break-throughs in late-twentieth-century medicine, i.e., reliable methods of pre-conception birth control. This story appears in Genesis 38:7–10, and tells of how the eldest son of Judah, named Er, was slain by the Lord because he was wicked. Thereupon Judah commanded his younger son, Onan, to perform the prescribed duty of a brother-in-law to Er's wife, Tamar. He was not only to provide her material support, but also to get her pregnant and to treat the progeny of this sexual union as the offspring of his dead brother. Knowing that the offspring would not be his own, Onan spilled his semen on the ground when he went in to his dead brother's wife, thereby depriving his deceased brother of any offspring. The story declares that Onan's behavior was displeasing to the Lord, so he too, was slain.

Ellens shows that the point of this story is not that coitus interruptus is inherently displeasing to God, but that Onan violated another fundamental law in the ancient Near East, a law that, like the law of hospitality, was designed to support the social order. In this case, the law had three pur-poses: preserving the name of a man who died young without progeny or heir; providing a clear line of legal inheritance for the estate of the dead man; and insuring that the widow had family to care for her in her advanc-ing years.

Ellens discusses the possible reasons why Onan refused to carry out this firmly established law—his brother was wicked, his wife was off-putting—and these explanations make a great deal of sense. What does not make any sense is that this "ridiculous story" has been used down through the centuries by Christians and Jews "as an argument for turning the very natural experience of masturbation into an evil behavior, even a terrifying sin against God" and has led to the even more damaging view, still officially promulgated by the Roman Catholic Church, "that sexual behavior is primarily for reproduction and that any sexual act which is used in any other way is a sin against God's will and design for humans."

Thus the Catholic Church's teaching on the so-called sin of onanism, i.e., masturbation and *coitus interruptus*, has resulted in its failure to lead "the world into a wise and wholesome course of action which could have approved and encouraged pre-conception birth control and forbidden abortion." In Ellens's judgment such a wise and judicious course, evidently envisioned by Pope John XXIII, would have gained the support of most Christian communities and prevented the intentional abortion of millions of unborn children in the United States and other Christian nations.

This conclusion leads to a fourth important learning: If the primary purpose of sexual behavior is not reproduction, then what is? That the answer Ellens offers to this question is not altogether surprising does not mean that it is trivial or mundane. Put simply, the purpose of sex is to foster love. When it does this it fulfills its purpose. Thus, for Ellens, the reason that we should give our full attention to the subject of sex in the Bible is that by doing so we will discover that the Bible is a book that grows, steadily and inexorably, in its esteem for love, culminating in the wonderfully lyrical elegy to love in Paul's letter to the church in Corinth (1 Cor. 13). As Ellens writes of this soaring testimonial to love: "One cannot read these lines, with an eye for love's truth, without feeling a transcendent connection with the heavenly and the eternal." This brings us back to the opening chapter of the book in which Ellens draws a connection between sex and spirituality. He suggests that they reflect the same desire, only in a different key.

A word about the general tone of this book: No one would dispute the fact that sex in the Bible is a serious subject. It is serious, in part, because the Bible itself takes the subject seriously. It is also serious because the passages in the Bible that refer to sex have been so badly misinterpreted throughout the history of Christianity, and these misinterpretations have wreaked great havoc in human lives. On the other hand, Ellens is well aware that sex has its amusing side, and he takes considerable pleasure in pointing out the intentional and unintentional humor in the biblical authors' treatment of the subject. His primary reference to Jesus' view on sexual matters is his account of our Lord's amusing response to the Sadducees, who hoped to put him on the spot with a question deriving from the law that got brother Onan into a heap of trouble.

I may be forgiven, then, if I include in this foreword a joke that bears on Ellens's observation that many young Catholic boys were admonished that if they masturbated they would go blind. I can personally attest to the fact that for many Protestant boys, the threat of blindness topped our list, too, with that of growing hairy hands following as a close second. Fortunately, the association of masturbation with mental illness had faded by that time. However, the joke I want to tell in this regard:

A father enters the bathroom to brush his teeth and he finds that his son, Billy, is already there. The father says in a stern and exasperated voice, "Billy, how many times do I have to yell at you not to play with that thing? If you keep doing that you could go blind!" Billy responds, "Hey, Dad, I'm over here."

Somewhere in Michigan a man who has written a book on *Sex in the Bible* is laughing as he reads this, for he is a man of great learning and great humanity, but as the reader of this book will certainly discover, he has a rich sense of humor, too.

The reader will also discover that this book's author loves his daughters, and that he therefore celebrates the fact that they live in a social world—unlike that of the daughters of Lot, David, and other biblical fathers—where women are not the property of men, yet manifest the deeper biblical truth that they are the very reflection—and delight—of their Creator. These daughters would not exist, however, without their mother, who is exemplary of the women whom Erik H. Erikson describes in his essay on the sayings of Jesus as "a most down-to-earth goddess of the hearth."[1]

As Ellens shows, there is a profound connection between sexuality and the search and longing for the transcendent, and there is an equally profound relationship between sexuality and the desire of the God of Israel to come down to earth and discover hospitality in the human hearth—and heart. And so the story of sex in the Bible is the story of the Christian faith itself.

Donald Capps—Thanksgiving Day 2005
Princeton Theological Seminary

PREFACE

More than three decades ago, psychologist Paul D. Cameron conducted a survey on how often the average person thinks about three of the most inscrutable phenomena in human experience: sex, religion, and death. He polled 3,416 people at the University of Louisville asking them what they were thinking about in the preceding five minutes.

His results? Young adults, age 18 to 25, think about *sex* at least once in any 10-minute period; middle-aged people, at least every 35 minutes; and people over 65, once an hour. Young adults think about *religion* once every 25 minutes; middle-aged people, once every 15 minutes; older people, every 10 minutes. Young people think about *death* every 25 minutes; old people every 15 minutes.

Though the figures may have shifted a tad in the intervening years, the basic fact remains, today and every day, that we humans are irrepressibly given to wrestling with the understanding of our sexuality, religion, and mortality, at both conscious and unconscious levels.

The theme of this affirmative and challenging book by J. Harold Ellens is captured in a line from the last chapter: "It is clear from the stories about sex in the entire Bible that the appropriate celebration of human sexuality brings a great sense of blessedness and wholeness to human beings; and conversely, the misuse or lack of it brings many forms of disaster: socially, psychologically, and spiritually."[1]

There is a widespread impression, both within and outside the Judeo-Christian tradition, that the Bible is down on sex. This opinion is scotched with enthusiastic pleasure by the author. He takes us through the pages of the Hebrew Bible and the New Testament with the skill of a seasoned tour guide, familiar with the terrain, schooled in its tortuous mysteries, and awake to the psychological subtexts the average eye fails to see. His objective? To demonstrate that "we often misread the Bible, particularly on what it has to say about sex."[2]

In the 15 chapters of this book, J. Harold Ellens introduces us, with crisp insight and fine touches of humor, to texts, interpretations, and events that cover three millennia of Judeo-Christian history. He take us on visits to Mosaic law-codes, prophetic literature, the Psalms, and historical writings, the gospels and epistles, to the ancient opinions of the Talmud and early church fathers, to the genius and limitations of Augustine and Jerome. He follows this up with astute observations on the momentous impact of the pronouncements and opinions on sexuality by church councils throughout the history of Christianity, and he introduces us to the probing insights of psychologists and theologians, such as Freud, Jung, Adler, Seward Hiltner, Otto Piper, and Pope John XXIII.

Ellens brings impressive credentials to the mission of this book. He is a biblical scholar, a clinical therapist with 50 years of experience, a pastor, an Army chaplain who served with the 1st Infantry Division, the 6th Infantry Division (light), and the 8th Infantry Division, in war and peace. He is an author or editor of more than 100 books, a wise tutor and counselor, and a prophetic critic who shoots straight, but always manages to dip his arrows of truth in honey. He speaks with academic authority, with psychological acuity, with pastoral empathy, and with a vernacular style that can appreciate everything from a "romp in the hay" to the exotic sexual laws of the book of Leviticus, and Jesus' views on sex.

There are things you will disagree with in this book. There are also things that you will shake your head over, wondering "why no one has ever told us this before." And there are things that you will enjoy with Ellens as he tips over one false image about sex in the Bible after the other.

Ellens's introductory chapter on "The Psychology and Spirituality of Sex," contains one of my favorite passages, worth the price of the book. It confirms my long-standing suspicion that the drive of sexuality and the drive toward spirituality are not unrelated phenomena in the economy of human spiritual, physical, and psychic makeup:

> Sexual experience and expression, like spiritual experience and expression, are moved and driven by a deep inner vital force in our personalities that prompts us to reach out for the kind of connection with the other that we intuitively believe will make us whole and complete, while making the other,

at the same time, rapturous and fulfilled. When that inner life-force reaches out from our psyches toward another human being in whom we delight, it arouses our physical being and channels its psycho-spiritual energies through our bodies toward communion and union with that other person. We call that sexuality. When that inner life-force reaches out from our psyches toward infinite transcendent reality, in our longing for God and eternity, we call it spirituality.[3]

In chapter 2, "The Bible, Sex, and Moralization," Ellens addresses the 20 centuries of overmoralized sex, stressing the point that it is not the Bible that has moralized sex; its interpreters have. The Bible takes sexuality as a matter of fact, as a source of human enjoyment and fulfillment, and as a staple reality of what it means to be human; just like eating, sleeping, hunting, gathering, building, and worshipping. To be sure, the Bible is concerned about the harmful misuse of sex, but in no sense does it share the puritanical preoccupation with sex as evil that has characterized so much of Western Christian thinking.

Chapter 3, "God's Sexuality: Deity, Gender, and Sexual Design in Creation," expands on a matter of exegetical and theological logic. Ellens argues that if, according to Genesis, male and female sexual humans are made in the image of God, it follows that God somehow shares in our sexuality and our maleness and femaleness. Somehow there is something about our sexual natures that reflects the creative and embracing nature of the reality at the heart of being, the reality in the essence of God.

In chapter 4, "Falling in and out of Love," Ellens puts on his pharmacological-clinical-psychological hat, providing a professional analysis of the biochemistry (e.g., phenylethylamine) of love at first site, but also the chemical factors at work in the phenomena of the "seven year itch" and the midlife crisis that often occurs later in the marriage cycle.

Chapter 5, on "Making Love: Celebrating Sex," introduces us to the storied voluptuousness of the Song of Songs, its celebration in Judaism and Christianity, and its eventual allegorical sanitization in the history of Jewish and Christian interpretation. Above all, this chapter introduces us to the quintessential role of sex in the biblical canon as a testimony to the divine goodness at work in the sexual embrace of two hearts, minds, and bodies, drawn to one another in love, in mutual enjoyment, and in a shared sense of responsibility for one another.

In chapter 6, "Making Babies: Purposes of Sex," Ellens provides an extensive, eye-opening account of how the significance of a single, brief story in Genesis 38:7–10 can be inflated, expanded, and misinterpreted to underwrite centuries of false teaching about sexuality in Western Christian tradition. The story tells us about Onan who "spilled his seed" rather than fulfill his responsibilities as a Levirate husband for his deceased brother's wife, a practice required by Levitical law. In Sherlock Holmes fashion, Ellens leads us through the historical evidence to show how this tale was allowed to become the proof text and basis for the sweeping and sustained condemnation of masturbation, birth control, and abortion over the centuries, by the Christian Church.

Chapter 7, on "Sin and Seduction: Adam, Eve and Sex Problems," introduces us to the fact that the book of Genesis contains two accounts for the origin of sin and evil. Looking at Genesis 3 and 6 through the lens of early intertestamental Jewish literature and pre-Judaic Mesopotamian creation stories, Ellens argues that in time, human "sin" was somehow wrongly traced to our nature as sexual beings, a misconception perhaps *implied* in the text, but certainly amplified by later interpreters, chief of whom was Augustine of Hippo. With keen psychological analysis of these classic stories, Ellens leads us to consider how they were distorted in later tradition and erroneously made to serve as evidence that sexuality is at the root of all evil. The chapter concludes with a survey of psychological approaches to this topic in the writings of Freud, Piaget, Erikson, and Hiltner.

Chapter 8 focuses on "Old Testament Sex Laws: Women as Property versus Women as Agents of Their Destiny," contrasting the later law codes on women found in Leviticus with the earlier ones in Deuteronomy. Chapter 9 turns to the topic of "Adultery: Sex and Marriage," noting the double standard on adultery reflected in many different biblical settings. Chapter 10 addresses the issues of "Monogamy: Models and Meanings," with the surprising thesis that although monogamy is not the biblical model, polygamy has rightfully come to be regarded both in Judaism and in Christianity as a less likely matrix for the fulfillment of individual, familial, and personal needs in the context of modern society.

Chapters 11 and 12 provide a probing psychological and biblical critical analysis of the six passages in the Hebrew Scriptures and New Testament that speak of homosexuality, spelling out how they were understood in their own historical context and how they are to be understood in the twenty-first century, looking back at these texts.

Chapter 13 is titled "Bad Sex," and points to a number of forms of sexuality explicitly forbidden by the Bible: incest, pedophilia, bestiality, necrophilia, rape, and sodomy. Ellens offers a sound proposal on how they are to be seen today in light of what we know of their psychological, physical, and social effects.

In the two closing chapters on "Sex and Love: The Real Thing," and on "Sex and Shalom: What God Had in Mind," Ellens puts on his counselor and pastoral hats, leading us to amplify our understanding of sex and love as "expressions of the heart of God."

Piet Hein, a Dutch poet and scientist, offers the following in one of his classic collections of "Grooks," poems with a point:

There was an old woman
Who lived in a shoe
She had so many children,
She didn't know what to do.
But try as she would
She could never detect
Which was the cause
And which the effect.[4]

The old woman's fundamental problem was not understanding how over-population can cause problems, but in bringing to consciousness an under-standing of the complexity, force, and quintessential character of sexuality as an inescapable force in her life. The purpose of *Sex in the Bible* is to serve as an antidote to that problem by introducing a new view of sexual-ity in the Bible that raises our consciousness of sexuality as a God-given endowment meant for communal, personal, and societal fulfillment.

Wayne G. Rollins
Thanksgiving Day 2005
Hartford, Connecticut

Chapter 1

INTRODUCTION: THE PSYCHOLOGY AND SPIRITUALITY OF SEX

The most fascinating thing about human beings is our irrepressible desire to make sense out of things. We have a deep hunger for meaning. From birth to death we press on with our quest to know and understand life and the world around us. We continually delve into the conscious and unconscious work of trying to know and understand each other and ourselves. Most of us make great gains in this life pilgrimage but none of us ever completes it. We can achieve a satisfying outlook on things during one lifetime but we never feel that we have finished the job and worked out the whole picture. There are always more questions to ask, more frontiers to cross, more spaces to be painted in on our intellectual and emotional canvass, more intriguing answers to be found. Indeed, most of us eventually come to realize that the more questions we are able to answer about the meaning of life, the more important questions are opened to us. We discover the answer to our question about whether we are loved and that prompts us to wrestle with the question as to what love really is. Our minds and hearts are insatiable in their quest for meaning. Eventually we realize that just getting the questions the right way around is often more important to our sense of meaning than getting all the answers worked out.

It is for all of these irrepressible reasons, I am sure, that Sacred Scriptures have an endless fascination for us. Our hunger for meaning is not just a quest to understand ourselves—it is a longing for a good grip on the ultimate nature of things: a longing for God and for a sense of eternity or transcendence. Our longing for the transcendent is a thirst for that which is beyond our selves, beyond the finite and material world, beyond our reach. Sacred Scriptures, in any faith-tradition, purport to wrestle with and reveal key insights about that transcendent dimension of things. Whether we revere the *Qur'an,* the *Hebrew Bible,* the *Bhagavad-Gita,* the *Analects* of Confucius, or the *Holy Bible,* which Christians revere, we tend to assume that its function is to provide us insights into God's nature, God's predictable behavior, God's relationship to us, and God's requirements of us. That is, we tend to assume that the body of literature we call our Sacred Scriptures puts us in touch with the transcendent perspective on our meaning quest. So we find such scriptures endlessly fascinating.

Moreover, our Sacred Scriptures have important cultural consequences. The cadences of their lines and thoughts, their poetry and proverbs, their messages and metaphors, insinuate themselves into our unconscious memories and so tend to be woven into the warp and woof of the literature, art, and symbols of our culture. They are mirrored in the values that shape our societies. It is impossible, for example, to read the plays and sonnets of William Shakespeare, or the essays of William Blake, or even to listen to much of the music of our own century's popular culture, with any significant degree of full understanding of it, unless we have a thorough knowledge of the Old and New Testament. The messages and metaphors of those Sacred Scriptures have crept into our literature at all levels and from every direction. Consciously and unconsciously those Sacred Scriptures shape our ways of thinking and feeling and valuing, because they are in the weave and pattern of our memory and our way of life, even if we do not personally avow any real allegiance to them.

That fact of life can be very constructive and very destructive. For example, the *Hebrew Bible,* which was produced by ancient Israelite religion, and the Christian writings that form the New Testament, were combined by a church council in 325 c.e. and together form the *Holy Bible.* These Sacred Scriptures have definitively shaped Western culture and society for the last 2,000 years. They are available to us today in a surprising variety of translations, versions, and paraphrases. I was raised on memorization of the King James Version (KJV) of the Bible. It was beautiful for its poetic style, but it has been greatly improved upon by the Revised Standard Version (RSV), a translation much closer to the original Hebrew Old Testament (OT) and Greek New Testament (NT). The KJV strongly influenced all of the great literature of the English-speaking world since the seventeenth century. Therefore, it has shaped our social and cultural values and outlook, whether we are conscious or unconscious of that. Today biblical scholars use the RSV because of its accuracy in translating the original languages.

For the purposes of this book, *Sex in the Bible,* we will depend upon the RSV exclusively, except in those cases in which I indicate that I have translated a passage directly from the original ancient Hebrew or Greek.

The Bible, as other Sacred Scriptures such as the *Qur'an,* has very helpful influences upon a society and culture when it insinuates into our hearts and minds those sentiments that lead to congenial relationships and constructive goals and ideals. When such scriptures reflect ancient models of enmity or violent motives and suggest that such styles and methods have divine approval, the effect upon our unconscious minds or our consciously chosen values can be very destructive. For example, the ancient Israelite religion that produced the *Hebrew Bible* (OT) gave the impression that our life and history is caught up in a cosmic conflict between God and the devil, good and evil, which is like a warfare carried out on the battlefields of history and the human heart.

This has led many Jews and Christians to believe that we are responsible to fight this battle against the enemies of God. It is easy for us to believe, apparently, that our enemies must be God's enemies. Since the *Qur'an* is also derived largely from the *Hebrew Bible,* Islam has adopted this same outlook on life. This kind of ancient metaphor shapes present-day societies and cultures and causes terrible violence and suffering. The worst thing about the notion of a cosmic conflict involving God and all humans is that it is a lie. No such battle is going on. There is no data for believing that such a thing exists. Evil is what humans do to each other, not the result of some cosmic evil force or devil.

Moreover, it has always been easy for people devoted to any Sacred Scripture to interpret its meanings and metaphors in erroneous ways not intended by the original writers and readers. Usually this misinterpretation of scriptures arises out of some human need to use the authority of Sacred Scriptures to support a private or institutional, political or religious idea, which the scriptures did not originally intend but for which we would like to assert an authoritative claim. This, for example, is what has happened in regard to sex in the Bible. For the last 20 centuries of Christian history, at least, there has been a tendency in Western society and culture to moralize human sexuality in an exaggerated way. At the same time, it has been our tendency to sexualize morality in a manner that has made it virtually the only issue of morality of which our society is aware.

This has resulted in two nearly humorous enigmas. First, it has split off our real social conduct from our official creed. While the society and culture make believe that we hold some norm of sexual decorum, most of the society constantly violates that norm and standard. Alfred Kinsey's published research,[1] the work of Masters and Johnson,[2] and other similar studies, such as *The Hite Report,*[3] indicate that approximately three-fourths of both men and women in America violate the official standards for sexual behavior in our society. Our super-moralization of sexuality has made us ethical and social schizophrenics, so to speak.

Second, our moralizing sexuality and sexualizing morality to an exaggerated degree has resulted in another kind of splitting. We seem to have sexualized morality to such a degree that there are no longer moral questions about anything other than sexual behavior on our ethical and spiritual radar screen. When the executives of Enron, for example, were caught with their very large hands in the very large corporate cookie jar, no one that I could find suggested that this was a moral or ethical question. Everyone seemed preoccupied with the fact that it was a legal and fiscal or accounting question.

On the other hand, when Nelson Rockefeller died of a heart attack in the bed of his mistress, or when Jesse Jackson acknowledged that he had a child out of wedlock, and when numerous Hollywood figures bore children without bothering to acquire husbands, our society tended to see these matters exclusively as issues of sexual morality and ethics. No one seemed to be prepared to ask how many years before his death Rockefeller's wife entered menopause, withdrew from the marriage relationship sexually, emotionally, socially, psychologically, aesthetically, and spiritually; and thus effectively violated and immorally terminated the marriage. I do not know that she did that, but it is one of the sociological and psychological questions of moral importance that must be asked in such a case, in addition to the one regarding Nelson's sexual morality. Not all sexual questions are moral issues and not all moral issues are sexual questions.

Moreover, no one seemed willing to ask how difficult it is for a busy professional woman, in Hollywood or elsewhere, to try to find a really good husband at age 36 who will not be part of her life-problem but part of her life-solution. Few people seemed willing to ask how much more manageable and authentic it may be for a busy working woman to contract to bear a child with a man whose genetics she admires, despite her knowledge that she could never effectively live with him. Better a joyful motherhood than a troubled marriage! The interesting thing is that the Bible comments on the Rockefeller-type case and we have repressed the message, while it does not comment on the Professional Woman case suggested above. Nonetheless, we generally presume in our society that we know very well what the constraints ought to be there, for the Rockefellers and the single movie-star mothers of our world.

It is my intention and desire to describe in this volume the notion that we often misread the Bible, particularly on what it has to say about sex. I should like to offer a new interpretation that allows for a fresh understanding of sex in the scriptures and in our lives. I believe there is a different, more helpful way of looking at what our revered scriptures have to tell us about human sexuality that can enlighten us regarding the real meaning and nature of sex. This work is, therefore, intentionally addressed to those in our society today who genuinely wish to know and understand more about what the Bible intends to say to us regarding the appropriate celebration of our sexuality and our sexual relationships. In this way I would like to lay a biblical foundation for overcoming the societal and cultural splitting and schizophrenia that seems to plague our world today, dividing our official sexual code from our society's sexual conduct.

This work is designed to discuss all aspects of human sexuality and the perspective offered by the numerous and varied authors of the 66 books of *the Holy Bible,* during the 1,000 years or so during which they wrote. Unfortunately, the Bible has been read, generally, through the screens of the church's dogma, theological interpretation, and moralizing framework for the last 2,000 years. I would like to try to see the Bible in its own right, as it was intended by its original writers to be understood by its original readers. If I can achieve that, this book will allow the biblical narrative to speak for itself, in its cultural and historical context. This will lead to comments upon how the original narrative has been interpreted subsequently throughout history. This treatment of the biblical material should make it possible to suggest insights about how the Old and New Testament message about sexuality has come to be understood today, by various communities of faith and practice in Judaism, Christianity, and Islam.

While the focus of this book is primarily upon Judaism and Christianity, it takes account of the fact mentioned above, that Islam and the teachings of the *Qur'an* are also derived from and influenced by the contents, particularly the stories, of the Bible. Hopefully that will allow us to determine how the Bible should speak to us about our sexuality today, in a social and psychological context very different from ancient times; though our spiritual context of longing for transcendental understanding and meaning may be very much the same as that of the original writers and readers of the Bible. It is my wish that this volume will engage the thoughtful reader who is serious about that sexual and spiritual quest.

Sexuality and spirituality are, after all, closely linked in the Bible and in our personal experience. It seems quite clear that both are expressions of our hunger for meaning and our longing for connection with the ineffable and transcendent dimensions of the human self. Sexual experience and expression, like spiritual experience and expression, are moved and driven by a deep inner vital force in our personalities that prompts us to reach out for the kind of connection with the other that we intuitively believe will make us whole and complete, while making the other, at the same time, rapturous and fulfilled. When that inner life-force reaches out from our psyches toward another human being in whom we delight, it arouses our physical being and channels its psycho-spiritual energies through our bodies toward communion and union with that other person. We call that sexuality. When that inner life-force reaches out from our psyches toward infinite transcendent reality, in our longing for God and eternity, we call it spirituality. That arouses our spirits in such a way as to channel our psycho-spiritual energy through our minds and hearts toward communion and union with the God we seek. This prompts us to expressions of meditation, song, prayer, and worship.

Whether we experience this expression of our inner life-force as sexuality or spirituality, much of the experience is the same. It is filled with aesthetic delight in the object of our affection, with celebration of what we imagine to be the perfections and wonders of the other, and produces an overflowing richness of emotion that gratifyingly exhausts our selves. It is not surprising that it is particularly regarding sexuality and spirituality that we use the same very special set of exquisite language: we speak of the progressing paradigm of experience from contact, to genuine encounter, to communication, connection, communion, union, ecstasy, and eternity. These terms have their very special meaning in just these two very special contexts, and the meaning in both spirituality and sexuality is the approximately same.

So here we are making the course-setting claim that spirituality is what we call the experience of our inner hunger for transcendent union with ultimate being, which we call God, and our reach for things godly. Sexuality is the name we accord that vital force or energy when it reaches out for union with "the other" on the horizontal level of humanness. The implication of this is plain. The Bible is a collection of writings about the human quest for meaning, particularly transcendent and eternal meaning; and about the meaning of the transcendent and eternal reality. This has to do with our life together before the face of God. Thus the Bible is inevitably a book that says a great deal about the nature and experience of sexuality. The Bible knows well and makes clear that sex is an integral part of the human spiritual quest, channeled through our psychological and physical machinery to connect us meaningfully with other humans, and through our psychological and spiritual machinery to connect us with God.

Chapter 2

THE BIBLE, SEX, AND MORALIZATION

The most interesting thing about sex in the Bible is the fact that the Bible does not moralize sex. It simply takes a matter-of-fact view of sex as a central human reality, like eating, sleeping, hunting, gathering, building, and worshipping. That is, the Bible thinks of sexuality as a common form of human creative expression. You could even say that the Bible simply thinks of sex as a valuable form of human communication and connection, and that is all there is to it. Of course, the Bible urges us to avoid some kinds of sexual behavior and assumes the normalcy of other kinds of sexual behavior. However, in each case, whether the Bible is for or against various kinds of sexual behavior, it is not on moral grounds but on the grounds that bad sex damages us and good sex is good for us, just like false worship undermines our authentic spirituality and true worship enhances our spirituality.

Moreover, it is clear when one takes the biblical view of sex as a whole, that the authors of the Bible were already aware of the intimate interaction between sexuality and spirituality, intuiting that when one exaggerates one side of that equation one shrinks and distorts the other side of the equation. When the mystics of the Middle Ages placed an overwhelming emphasis upon the repression of their sexuality for spiritual reasons, they exaggerated spiritual expression to the point of psychotic visions and ideations. In our day in the Western world the emphasis upon finding life's meaning almost completely in sexuality has been so overdrawn that the human quest for gratifying spirituality has been seriously truncated in our society and culture. This has led to bizarre obsessiveness and compulsivity in the pursuit of exaggerated distortions of the normal sexual union and communion that makes one feel whole and complete in love. Thus, if we distort either sexuality or spirituality, it causes a comparable distortion in the other. If we are preoccupied with spirituality at the expense of the repression of sexuality, our spirituality becomes sick and exaggerated, inauthentic. If we are preoccupied with sexuality at the expense of the repression of our spirituality, our sexuality becomes sick and distorted, unreal and unnatural.

Unfortunately, the church has spent the better part of 20 centuries overmoralizing sex. There is no biblical foundation for this. If one asks why this should have happened, the only way an answer can be found is that either powerful authorities in the early church were uncomfortable about their own sexuality and projected their pathology upon Christian theology and ethics; or the bishops realized very early that overmoralizing sexual behavior offered an enormous tool for control of the constituency of the church. The power of this tool of control, of course, would have lain in the fact that it was a way to keep everybody full of fear, guilt, and shame. Having cast things in that mold, control of the parishioners was much easier. Thus church attendance and church income could be maintained at high levels. High church attendance could be maintained as a requirement for forgiveness and absolution. High church income could be maintained as a by-product of the formula for relieving troubled consciences. Moreover, the fear of transgression, and fear of the accompanying guilt and shame, imposed a certain repressive control on social behavior in any society.

Probably the matter got off on the wrong foot early in the history of Christianity because of the overwhelming influence St. Augustine and St. Jerome had upon the shape of things from the fourth century onward. St. Augustine was a celibate leader from the time of his adult conversion to Christianity. This was an overreaction to the first half of his life, which he lived as a pagan and lascivious libertine. He spent the rest of his life in confession of his sins, dedicating his life to pristine abstinence. He admired the celibate hermits of Egypt and died as a bishop who influenced the character of the Christian Church more than any other person.

St. Jerome's influence was similar. He was a practicing homosexual before his conversion, as an adult, to the Christian faith. Homosexual behavior was not abnormal in Greek and Roman society of that time. However, when he converted to Christianity he interpreted some of St. Paul's writings as forbidding homosexuality. He felt great guilt. Then when he was found in a compromising situation on two or three different occasions after his conversion, he was overwhelmed with fear, guilt, and shame. He moved to Bethlehem, built a monastery, and lived the rest of his life there with a large coterie of Christian widows. He produced an enormous amount of scholarship on translation and interpretation of the Bible and wrote much in favor of the Egyptian hermit "saints." He is probably the one who influenced the church to eventually require celibacy for its clergy.

However important the influence of St. Jerome and St. Augustine may have been in heading the church down the road toward overmoralizing sexuality, it remains very clear that the posture of the church on this matter for the last 20 centuries does not square with the message of the Bible on human sexuality. The Bible does not make a large matter out of the issue of human sexual behavior. It avoids casting the subject into such contrasting categories as natural behavior versus social convention, or sacred versus secular behavior, or holy spirituality versus earthy sexuality. The Bible simply assumes that sexuality is an important part of our normal function as image bearers of God. It treats sexuality as a matter of human relationship and not essentially as an issue of genital behavior. Moreover, it keeps sexuality and spirituality closely linked in human personality.

The Bible specifies a few, indeed a very few, sexual behaviors that it abhors as destructive to human nature. It does not even comment overtly upon the wide world of normal sexual play between consenting adults, married or unmarried. Sexuality in the Bible is about close cherishing communion and intimate mutuality between two persons and no standard form is suggested, to say nothing of being prescribed. Aside from those few sexual behaviors which are proscribed, that is, forbidden, there is no form of "conformity" that is idealized, or of nonconformity that is marked out as "tragic" or "sinful."

We ought to let the Bible speak for itself once again, particularly on such central matters as sexuality and spirituality. To achieve that valuable objective, it will be helpful to look carefully at the nature of the Bible itself, and at the kinds of literature we have in these 66 books that have been of so much help to so many people in so many ways for so long a time.

We may start that exploration by observing, of course, that the Bible does not intend to be a textbook on human sexuality or on any thing else, for that matter. Nor does the Bible pretend to lay down any significant authoritative science of social or sexual morality or ethics. The Bible is a collection of literary works of various types, which were written, edited, and reedited over a period of about 1,100 years, from the time that David wrote some of the Psalms around 1,000 B.C.E. until the New Testament was completed about 100 C.E.

Most of the *Hebrew Bible* or Old Testament was thoroughly reedited during or after the exile of the Israelites in Babylon between 586 and about 200 B.C.E. Most of the *Hebrew Bible* was written in Hebrew, but some parts of it, such as chapters in Daniel, were written in Aramaic, Jesus' mother tongue. The whole of it was translated into Greek in Alexandria, Egypt, sometime between 150 and 50 B.C.E. The Epistles of Paul were written between 65 and 75 C.E., while the Gospels were apparently written between 75 and 110 C.E.

The variety of literature in the Bible is quite remarkable and very interesting. Some of the Bible, for example Genesis 1 to 11, is made up of ancient stories derived largely from Babylonian and Zoroastrian lore, told and retold, until they were finally put down in writing in a perspective that comported well with Israelite faith and religious practice. Other large sections of the Bible are an attempt at recording historical events. Parts of Deuteronomy, Joshua, Judges, the Books of the Kings, and the Chronicles would fall into that category. While such works as Ruth and Esther aspire to something of historical status, they are likely to be more of a mythic quality. This is true of much of the Bible. However, it must be understood that "mythic" in this sense does not mean "untrue" or "fairy tale" or mere "legend." The proper use of the term *myth* in this kind of context means a piece of literature or a narrative which has more of the quality of a confession of faith than of a literal empirical record of historical data. Ruth and Esther are probably books that have a core of historical truth at the center and then build a story around those cores. In this way they make a claim for an important spiritual or religious truth.

For example, the core of the Esther story is in the fact that she persuaded the king to give up his anti-Semitism and forbid it in his kingdom. The fact that she did this by sexually seducing him may or may not be part of the core of the history. It is not important regarding the outcome of the story, nor does the story make a judgment about her behavior. It approves the outcome and has become an important mythic component in Israelite cultural and religious lore. In like manner, the story of Ruth may well have at its core some history about an Israelite family becoming enmeshed with Moabites. The point of the story, however, is not about that but about the religious and spiritual reality of Ruth's abject devotion to Naomi and the God of Israel. Whether this is historical is beside the point. That it represents or expresses a profound truth about human relationship is the issue. Thus it is a confessional statement, a spiritual myth, a godly truth that gives meaning to our lives. Much of the Bible must be seen as that type of literature.

In addition to historical literature, legend, and mythic narratives, the Bible contains a great deal of poetry, most of it quite dramatic, and some of it designed to be read or acted out on stage, as in the case of the Book of Job. All of the Psalms are songs to be sung in the congregations' worship services: chants, choral readings, antiphonal songs, unison songs, and the like. Some are songs of lament, some of praise, some of prayer and petition, and some are songs and readings that recall the mighty acts of God in Israel's historical and spiritual journey, as persons or as a people. The 50 or so references to sex in the Bible are rather inadvertent remarks, incidental to the unfolding of these various kinds of literature and historical memory.

Such sections of the *Hebrew Bible* as the books of Ezra and Nehemiah attempt fairly straightforward history about the exile in Babylon and the return of some Israelites to Jerusalem. These are related, however, to such books of prophecy as Zechariah, Isaiah, Jeremiah, Ezekiel, and Daniel. These are largely books of sermons, comments, or pronouncements on certain events in history that are happening at the time of these prophetic commentators. They, like the poetic books of Job, Ecclesiasties, and Proverbs, are designed to teach important requirements of social order or theology. The remaining prophetic books do the same in more general ways. That leaves the Old Testament book of the Song of Songs or the Song of Solomon, which is lovely poetry, written, apparently, for the sole purpose of celebrating the joy of sex. The theme of sex is treated simply throughout the Bible, but is also irrepressibly present throughout.

The literature that makes up the New Testament tends to fall into the same categories as that of the *Hebrew Bible*. The gospels are stories that tend to use the narrative of the life of Jesus of Nazareth as a framework for making a number of points about theology, spirituality, and social psychology. The Acts of the Apostles purports to give us a history of the very early Jesus Movement, with a good deal of theological commentary upon it. The Pauline Epistles, those actually written by Saul of Tarsus and those put out later by others, but under Paul's name, as well as the Epistles by Peter and John, are all about the theological meaning of the stories of the gospels. The Book of the Revelation of St. John is largely poetry and attempts a very mythic philosophy of history designed to give the church hope during a Roman persecution that was designed to exterminate Christianity altogether.

Woven throughout these various kinds of biblical literature are the references to human sexuality. Rarely are these references of a legal or instructional nature. Moreover, the Bible says much more about sex by what it omits saying overtly than by what it specifically expresses. In the books of Leviticus and Deuteronomy, for example, as we shall see in chapter 8, the Bible specifically forbids certain sexual behaviors. In his Epistle to the Romans, St. Paul calls certain homosexual behavior an evil thing. But the amazing thing about the Bible's view of sex is how infrequent are such normative statements and what a narrow range of sexual behaviors are forbidden. For the most part, the Bible simply assumes that a universal and lively activity of natural sexual play is constantly going on between consenting adults.

It is surprising that the wide range of normal and healthy sexual play between consenting adults, within and outside of marriage, hardly comes up for comment anywhere in the Bible. The only place that sexual experience is directly related to the marriage bond is in Hebrews 13:4 where we read, "Let marriage be held in honor among all, and let the marriage bed be undefiled; for God will judge the immoral and the adulterous." This is a "stand-alone statement" in a list of directives regarding social behavior, emphasizing the importance of: brotherly love, hospitality to strangers, care of the underprivileged, avoiding adultery, resisting preoccupation with money, and reverence to leaders. All these have to do with inner integrity and outer decorum. They could be summarized in one sentence: "Do not betray or neglect the other or yourself."

Sexuality is, incidentally, just one of those ordinary cases in which one might be in danger of such betrayal or neglect. Adultery, for example, is less about sexuality or sexual behavior and more about protecting the marriage contract. It declares that if one is married one must protect the integrity of that contract. A spouse who withdraws from the normal emotional, spiritual, and sexual union inherent to marriage is as guilty of violating and terminating that marriage contract as is a spouse who engages in a sexual relationship with a partner other than the rejecting and alienating spouse.

It is not surprising, in the light of the above, that certain specific questions continue to arise in our minds about the biblical view of sex. Is polygamy wrong, and if so, why is it the prevailing model throughout the Bible? Does the Bible really mean that sexual love between two people of the same gender is wrong, even though they were born with homosexual orientation? Was sexual behavior really intended originally only for creating new lives, and if so, how could the Song of Songs celebrate sexual play between two apparently unmarried lovers just for the fun of it? Did the Bible, at a distance of 3,000 years from today, have some kind of principle in mind in forbidding bad sex, or did it simply agree with our judgment that certain kinds of sexual behavior are bad because they are destructive, and some kinds are even criminal?

This book is designed to answer these and many other relationship questions dealing with our understanding of the teaching of the Bible regarding sex. Our understanding about what the Bible has to say about sex has often been misguided, inappropriately theologically biased, and designed for repressive control. However, the Bible is primarily oriented, so far as possible, toward freedom, creativity, and joyful self-expression in everything in life, even in our sexuality. In this volume I hope to achieve a more balanced outlook by consulting our Sacred Scriptures themselves. What did they mean to the people who wrote them and the original audience that heard or read them? Did those folks have the correct take on these issues? How should we read or hear these Sacred Scriptures today, in the context of our complex cultural times? Can we get a correct take on them ourselves?

I would like you to walk through the biblical narratives with me and listen to how the biblical messages have been interpreted in different contexts, thereby discerning, perhaps, some new ways of reading these passages and translating them into our own lives. We can acquire fuller understanding of what the essential questions about human sexuality really are, how we may seek and find some of the answers, and how we may see a variety of sexual practices, and sexuality in general, through a new lens in a new light.

To do this efficiently I have included quotations from the scripture within the text of this book, rather than just referring to this or that section of the Bible cryptically, such as John 3:16, and forcing the reader to look them up separately or go on reading without a specific knowledge of what the Bible really says in a given instance about a specific matter. I have found personally, that nothing is quite so exasperating as reading a book in which there are a lot of scripture texts cited and none are written out. If you have no Bible available in which to look them up, you are stuck with only a vague knowledge of what the author is working on. If you do have your Bible with you but are in an airplane or in some other setting with limited table space, it can be very annoying and awkward to be forced to look up the reference or go on without precise knowledge of the text being discussed. In this volume they are all quoted within the text to make things easier and more effective for everyone.

Chapter 3

GOD'S SEXUALITY: DEITY, GENDER, AND SEXUAL DESIGN IN CREATION

One of the most curious references to sex in the Bible strongly suggests that God is sexual.[1] Genesis 1:22–27 reports God saying, "Let us make humans in our image, after our likeness. . . . So God created humans in God's own image, in the image of God he created them, male and female." This is essentially the translation one finds in the Revised Standard Version of the Bible, except that I have translated the Hebrew word "adam" as human rather than man. That word, as it is used in this passage, intends to refer to all humanity, in both genders. Obviously the Bible intends to tell us that there is something essential to the very nature of God which is reflected in human gender and sexuality. No wonder the Song of Songs can celebrate human sexuality with such joyous freedom and abandon. Sex is obviously God's thing, and the godly thing for humans.

So the high value and import of human maleness and femaleness is asserted in the Bible in its very first comment about these matters. Gender and sexuality are of God and are reflective of the very nature of God in us. The Bible might have said a number of other things at this juncture that would have surprised us less and seemed more certainly to be true. For example, we should have considered it quite understandable had the Bible said in Genesis 1: 27, "So God created humans in his own image . . . intellectual and rational;" or had it said, "So God created humans in his own image . . . emotional and spiritual." The author of Genesis might even have written, "So God created humans in his own image . . . praying and worshipping creatures, or loving and caring people." What would have really impressed me is if the author of Genesis had said, "So God created humans in his own image . . . proficient in developing and using imaginative language." All those we would readily have understood.

Nonetheless, the Bible tells us that the characteristics of God's nature reflected in us are not primarily our spirituality, rationality, intellectual or emotional excellence, or language proficiency; but our gender, our sexuality, our maleness and femaleness. It is in the sexual nature of humans and of God that we are so similar to God, so godlike. Theologians have wrestled for centuries with what Genesis 1:27 can possibly mean. In what sense is God sexual? What does that say about God? How does that define him? Is that merely a human term with which we try to refer to some important characteristic in God, or does that somehow actually define his nature? What does that say about him and, therefore, about us?

Whenever we try to speak about God in any way at all, of course, we must always speak in metaphors. We have available to us only word pictures that reflect our human world and are drawn in terms of things, experiences, and relationships familiar to us. That is, we can only ever speak of God in ways that are to some degree anthropomorphic, crafted in terms of human ideas and images. Does that mean that we have made God in *our* own image in Genesis 1:26–27? The Bible insists that God has made us in *his* image. It would be easy to humanize that passage, turn its message on its head, and conclude that associating our sexuality metaphorically with God's nature is merely anthropomorphic. There are many interpreters of the Bible who have done just that.

However, the issue at stake here has to do with what we lose if we reduce the Bible to mere anthropomorphic metaphors. It is clear that the author of this passage, and related passages elsewhere in the Bible, could have said that God is like us, but he or she clearly intended to put it the other way around. In our sexual natures we are like God. What did that ingenious writer intend? Was it his or her intent to say that within God there is an exotic erotic force that drives God irrepressibly and insatiably to desire himself, as we desire each other sexually? Did the writer intend that within God is such a pleroma of fullness and multiplicity that each aspect of God longs for every other aspect of God as we long for sexual union and the sense of wholeness or completeness such union brings us? That would give us some kind of explanation of why the text refers to God in the plural in Genesis 1:26–27. It refers to God as *Elohim*, whereas the singular would have been the Hebrew word *El*, used throughout the rest of the first chapter of the Bible and frequently elsewhere.

Perhaps Genesis 1 intends to say even more than that about God's nature, and our own. Is it possible that we should read this passage as saying the

God desires us and longs for communion and union with us in some way comparable to how we desire and long for each other sexually? I suppose that is highly likely. At least we might suppose that we have here a reference to the fact that God has an irrepressible need to connect and communicate within himself as well as with us and his created world; and that our gender polarity and our sexual polarity both incite us to that same kind of spontaneous and hungry reach for encounter, contact, communion, and union with another person or with other persons; as our need is the same as that need which is present in the very nature of God.

Moreover, being made in God's image, namely, male and female, must surely mean that just as God is the creator of life, so he has designed us to be creators of life. By declaring that God created us in his image, the text surely means to say that God reproduced himself and made us persons who reproduce ourselves. However, it is clear that God made the entire organic creation in his image, in that sense. Almost all creatures and plants reproduce through gender polarity. That is one of the truly remarkable things about whole the created world.

Furthermore, while that intensity of sexual attraction is a central part of the design by which God evolved the whole world, there must be something more than that irrepressible capacity for reproduction that is referred to here in Genesis 1:27. If the text did not mean something more than that, and something more special than that, why would it have made the special point that it is only the human organism, in its sexuality, that is imaging God? Does not the whole organic world do the same? Something about human sex is special in a godlike way! What could that be?

Perhaps, at the heart of this question, lies the fact that God created us with the capacity to express both our intense, irrepressible, raw, unconscious, libidinal sexual desire for each other and, at the same time, our conscious and thoughtful decision about when, where, why, how, and with whom to fashion that cherishing communion and union that makes us feel like whole persons. Thus, there is something about our sexual natures that reflects God's nature, in that our sexual behavior is primarily for creating cherishing relationships of love and caring kindness, not primarily for reproduction as in all the rest of the organic world. Human sex is special. Yes, it can implement reproduction, but that is ancillary to the creation of a quality life of love and union, joy and wholeness, peace and tranquility.

I suppose one could make an additional observation, which is probably peripheral rather than central. If human sex is for joyful cherishing, why did God make it so irrepressible? Moreover, why did God connect our sexuality to reproduction? Furthermore, why did God connect sexuality and reproduction to the function of our genitals? These are more entertaining than enlightening questions, I fear. God could have designed us in such a way that sexual polarity was not necessary for reproduction. God could have given us an insatiable longing for each other, thus insuring our communion and union for the sake of our sense of wholeness, without tying that longing for union to either our genitals or to reproduction. There are a few organisms in our world which reproduce all by themselves, without gender differences.

God might have rigged things in such a way that we would have the strong desire for union with each other but cause reproduction to take place without union, each of us reproducing ourselves by ourselves. If it was important for pregnancy to be based on gender difference and our union as two people with different sexual orientation, it could have been designed to take place simply by a hand shake or a kiss, rubbing noses or elbows. Moreover, it might have been implemented, in such a case, without any reference to genital function or behavior. Presumably, it could have been designed by God in such a way that even then sex, union, reproduction could all have been as delicious and delightful an experience in all of those ways, as they are now with genital heterosexual unions.

However, the case is that gender polarity is employed to implement sexual longing, and that in turn is linked to the desire that produces emotional and spiritual union, as a result of which sometimes reproduction takes place, and it always takes place with genital behavior involved. I imagine that the linking of gender, sex, cherishing, emotional union, and reproduction had a pragmatic motive behind it. It ensured that men reach out for women even when they prefer to go hunting and fishing, because their desire for sex, union, and cherishing is irrepressible. Likewise, women reach out for men even when they would rather run off to the office or nurse the baby, because their desire for sex, union, and cherishing is irrepressible. This keeps the relationship healthy. When the sex is good all the big problems seem like little ones. When sex is inadequate all the little problems seem like big ones.

I suppose, further, that God linked reproduction to these strong longings and irrepressible desires because that was a handy pragmatic way to ensure the survival of the human race during more primitive times when hunting and fishing and tending the garden probably really were more crucial to survival and more fun than trying to support more children. Undoubtedly the linkage of all this to our genitals was another stroke of sheer pragmatic ingenuity. When you consider the miracle of conception, gestation, and birth, and particularly the manner in which the organs involved are designed to facilitate all that while protecting the baby in the womb from danger of infection and invasive organisms, sealed off from external threats until the very moment of entering the birth canal, the only conclusion to be drawn is that this arrangement is an amazing feat of practical design and function.

Another aspect of the biblical narrative that bears on the issues of gender, at least, if not sexuality, has to do with the fact that God is referred to most of the time in the Bible as a patriarchal male, that is, a masculine figure in a role like that of the king or head of a large household, in this case the household of the people of Israel (OT), or of the entire world of humans (NT). Almost certainly this is a direct result of the fact that the idea of God and his nature, as perceived in the Bible, developed originally in a culture that was dominated by the notions of kingship and patriarchal households that prevailed at that time, 3000–500 B.C.E.

In that sense, referring to God as a male is in some ways an anthropomorphism, making God in the image of human cultural concepts. However, one cannot use that argument in one place when it suits one, and not in another place when it does not, unless there is good data dictating those choices. When God is referred to in the Bible as though God is male in gender, the notion can be a real problem for people who have grown up with fathers who have been reprehensible. How can you love God deeply and spontaneously when the image of him given by the Bible is that of a father, while in your heart of hearts you harbor deep wounding, grief, rage, and terror associated with your father? The feminist and womanist movements, which have pointed this out, have a legitimate case to make and it must be taken seriously. Producing inclusive language editions of the Bible for use in worship, such as the New Revised Standard Version (NRSV), is useful, even though they are not precisely and literally accurate reflections of the original text of the Bible. They are in many instances true to the spirit of the Hebrew and Greek texts, nonetheless.

However, that is not the entire or even the central issue at stake here. It is true that the Bible represents God as our father. Most human beings have had a good experience with their fathers. For most of us, therefore, the image of God as our father produces deep unconscious and conscious feelings of trust, honor, love, cherishing, gratitude, and security. Associating those ideas with God leads us directly along the road to wholesome spirituality and an anticipation of God's embracing grace and cherishing love. It leads us to a sense of wholeness and security about life and eternity. Thus, the image of God as father in the Bible is more than a mere anthropomorphism. It is a real fact that God fathers us and his whole creation, in sustaining providence and forgiving grace, and that it is that experience that makes all the difference in the world.

It is a good thing that God is our father, and that that fact is not just a word or a metaphor. In his being he is our father. But God is also our mother. That is, to limit God to one gender would be absurd. The image of God expressed in us is "male and female" according to Genesis 1:27. That has a lot of implications. First of all, all of us have some qualities of maleness and femaleness in us. Both are natural. All of us also have some heterosexual and some homosexual needs. By the time we finish negotiating the shoals of puberty we normally settle down solidly in one orientation or the other, but we retain both in some degree. People who are intensely negative toward homosexuality usually are reacting to larger-than-comfortable homosexual needs in themselves, which they are repressing aggressively into their subconscious. The clinical data in this regard is quite clear. We call it homophobia, fear of homosexuality, in ourselves.

God is our mother. The Bible says so. In the prophet we hear God declaring that she has dandled her people on her knee as a mother dandles her child, thrusting her ample milky breast into the hungry mouths of her needy children (Isaiah 66:11–13). Jesus wept over the waywardness of Jerusalem, saying (Matthew 23:37), "How often would I have gathered your children together as a hen gathers her chickens under her wings. . . !" God, as a chicken? A mother hen? That is Jesus' own metaphor. God's own self-designation? A mother with milky breasts, maternal knees, a mother's tenderness, and thoughtful compassion? Indeed! God fathers us and mothers us.

Those are not just good metaphors, nice words, but real being and nature in God, the God in the Bible. It is interesting that in spite of the dominating patriarchal culture of the biblical times, these passages come through, nonetheless, with this image of God as our mother. God is not male or female, but God combines all that is characteristic of our two genders and more than that: father, mother, brother, sister, lover, and friend. That is what the Bible intends to say, and that is what is carried into its first great reference to our natures: we are crafted in God's image—male and female, full of passion, love, and sex!

So it is especially in our sexual nature that our spiritually transcendent and godlike qualities are evident. However, human sexuality is more than mere copulation. In our better moments we think of human sexual relationship as making love. It is interesting what a difference it makes, for example, in the inner world of feeling and the outer connection of a relationship to hear your spouse or lover say, "Let's make love," as compared with hearing a person say, "Let's have sex." The difference lies in the fact that the communion and union of lovers is so much more than "having sex." It is the deep cherishing connection of two people in the sensual, emotional, social, psychological, and spiritual dimensions of our personalities.

Making love is a way of life. It is the tone with which one lives the day in tenderness and anticipation. In that sense the whole day is foreplay. How you joke when you awaken, disheveled from a night of deep sleep; how you touch at breakfast in appreciation of the moment; how you say goodbye and hello; how you speak while the day unfolds, the tone of your sensitivity and humorful joy all day long, all life long, is as much "making love" as the "roll in the hay" when the actual opportunity for intercourse finally presents itself. When this life of foreplay is absent, sexual love easily deteriorates into merely "having sex." That soon deteriorates into not having sex; and alienation follows.

The communion and union is missing, it brings no wholeness and completeness, it can easily make one feel more lonely, isolated, distant, and utterly alone in the things that really count in lives of real relationship. Merely having sex may be little more gratifying than masturbation, with the emptiness, incompleteness, and loneliness that usually follow that. Moreover, if the sexual relationship remains at the primitive level of mere encounter, contact, and connection; and does not develop into a real communication, communion, and union, real ecstasy is quite unlikely to be achieved, as the total absorption of two lovers in each other, the ideal experience of falling in love and of making love.

Chapter 4

FALLING IN AND OUT OF LOVE

One of the most delicious and excruciating human experiences is falling in love. One of the most heart-wrenching and ultimately freeing processes is falling out of it. There are good reasons for both and they have only indirectly to do with making love or achieving meaningful sexual union. All of us want to be in love, unless we have some significant psychological or social pathology. Some persons may not feel at all that they would like to be in love. This may be because they are afraid of intimacy or responsibility in relationship; or they may be worn out by a discouraging experience in which they really invested themselves. They may be depressed about life and lack the optimism and motivation that desiring love requires. They may have a pinched and constricted personality because of inherited shyness or a lousy home life as children. The models of relationships they have experienced may have poisoned their normal longing for the interest, intrigue, and excitement of being in love. Any and all of these are forms of sickness of the mind and spirit.

Normal healthy persons want to be in love. Whether they are 14 or 94, male or female, human beings would like to be in love. Being in love is a special kind of emotional experience that involves the awakening of the whole person, body, mind, and spirit. It feels like it starts in the very center of our souls and radiates out into our psyches, minds, feelings, and bodies. It is a response to some mysterious stimulant that characterizes or is a characteristic of the object of our being in love. Psychologists and sociologists have spent a great deal of time and put down a very lot of ink trying to figure out what those stimuli are; and why they empower us with that electric feeling of being in love.

Cole Porter sang out the mysterious theme and jerked the heartstrings of every one of us. "What is this thing called love?," he sang, and the world sang with him and long after him. Some wag suggested the numerous ways you can punctuate the question. "What is this thing called? Love?" or "What? Is this thing called love?" However you ask it, the joyfully exciting mystery remains.

> However punctuated, Cole Porter's simple question begs an answer. Love's symptoms are familiar enough: a drifting mooniness in thought and behavior, the mad conceit that the entire universe has rolled itself up into the person of the beloved, a conviction that no one on earth has ever felt so torrentially about a fellow creature before. Love is ecstasy and torment, freedom and slavery. Poets and songwriters would be in a fine mess without it. Plus it makes the world go round.[1]

Because "God created humans in his own image, in the image of God he created them; male and female." (Genesis 1:26–27). Amazing! What is it about being in God's image that does these wonderful, mysterious, and painful things to us?

Some think that we are stimulated to the deep earthy chemistry reactions of being in love by seeing characteristics of our love objects that unconsciously remind us of the way our mothers or fathers looked when we saw them in our helpless infancy from the crib. Others associate the reaction of being in love with smells, sounds, body shapes, auras of virility or fertility, or cherishing responses that give us a deep sense of peace we seldom experience and perpetually long for. Most researchers and commentators on these experiences think that the triggers are mostly unconscious and that our reasons for reacting to them as we do are unconscious as well.

If we take the Song of Songs as an expression of such chemistry and electricity of falling in love, we must conclude that the buttons that turn us on are physical, intellectual, emotional, and spiritual. Those buttons are olfactory, gastronomic, religious, and aesthetic, that is, they have to do with how our love objects smell, taste, respond to us, and how they sense the meaning of things. The things that stimulate us have to do with the powers of thought our lovers evince, and the way in which they appreciate the beauty of things all around us, including especially the beauty of cherishing sensitivity to our presence, words, desires, values, and longings. Often it seems that when we fall in love our lover senses our meanings before we finish expressing them, and completes our sentences before we get to the end, and knows what we are feeling before we can say it. Falling in love is delicious and often such an intense longing as to be painful.

Now, we all are quite sure we know exactly what is happening when we are falling in love. We are simply falling in love. We see it as a scintillating experience of romance. There is nothing so mysterious about it. The object of our love is a person with so many marvelous characteristics that we could continue the list of them all day and all night long. The delightful qualities of our love object are infinite in number and inexhaustibly exciting. There is no need to question what it is like, how it comes about, how it works, or where it is leading. It is simply wonderful and that is all there is to it. Any one who does not know all that automatically has simply never been in love and is hopelessly and helplessly ignorant of this whole wonderful world of exotic human reality.

After all, when you see a magnificent rose blossom, in all its splendid beauty, no one needs to tell you what it means that the beauty is thrilling and unimaginably heavenly. It just is. Do not ask too many questions. Stand back and let it be. Admire it from afar or near, but do not try to examine it too closely, lest you invade its beauty and break its petal, marring its magnificence. For God's sake, do not take the gorgeous rose into the laboratory and start to examine it scientifically. What good can possible come of that? So you dissect it, you dye its parts, you cook its inner filaments, and chemically analyze it. Then what do you have. All the beauty is gone. There is no rose left. You simply have nothing left in your hand. You know everything about nothing and who really cares, now that all the beauty is gone.

Dissecting a rose to discover the reasons for its beauty is a little like Suzanne Massie's story about the Communist experiment in the Soviet Union.[2] She describes the blossoming beauty of Old Russia, from the tenth to the early twentieth century. Her report on the extraordinary development of the professional arts, the carefully designed urban quality of the great cities, and the infinite richness and skill of the rural arts and crafts is nothing short of stunning. She saw Old Russia as an exemplary society with a profoundly artistic soul. The difficulty with it was the fact that the professional arts and quality urban life was mainly accessible to the elegant elite and educated citizens. Much of the general citizenry lived on a subsistence level of meager hope and very limited possibilities.

When the Communists came it was their avowed plan and intent to universalize the good life for all the citizenry of that great land. But 60 years into the Communist experiment, when Massie wrote her book, not only had the quality of the life of the citizenry not improved, but, unfortunately, all the majestic former beauty was gone. Sometimes we feel that when our experience of falling in love is examined too closely in order to understand what it is we are experiencing, something happens a little like the rose in the laboratory and the Communist experiment in the USSR. Holding it too close to the light does not always illumine love. Sometimes it simply evaporates it.

Consequently, after avoiding research on our experiences of falling in and out of love for a long time, scientists have taken a new look at this universal and mysterious aspect of our humanness.

> The reason for this avoidance, this reluctance to study what is probably life's most intense emotion, is not difficult to track down. Love is mushy; science is hard. Anger and fear, feelings that have been considerably researched in the field and the lab, can be quantified through measurements: pulse and breathing rates, muscle contractions, a whole spider's web of involuntary responses. Love does not register as definitively on the instruments: it leaves a blurred fingerprint that could be mistaken for anything from indigestion to a manic attack. Anger and fear have direct roles—fighting or running—in the survival of the species. Since it is possible (a cynic would say commonplace) for humans to mate and reproduce without love, all the attendant sighing and swooning and sonnet writing have struck many pragmatic investigators as beside the evolutionary point.[3]

In trying to understand the human experience of falling in and out of love, we might speculate about which came first, love or sexual desire. Are we driven mostly by the deep-seated need to reproduce or by the equally primal need to cherish and celebrate each other intimately? Have the poets and playwrights teased us into idealized notions of romance or are we inherently helpless before the surges of our inner longings? How do rational people flood euphorically into the elysian fields of utterly mindless obsession with someone who, when looked upon in the broad light of day, so to speak, is not, in point of fact, all that extraordinary?

> When people in love come to their senses, they tend to orbit with added energy around each other and look more helplessly loopy and self-besotted. If romance were purely a figment, unsupported by any rational or sensible evidence, then surely most folks would be immune to it by now. Look around. It hasn't happened. Love is still in the air.[4]

Gray winds up his lyrical commentary about human love and sexual attraction by suggesting that trying to figure out love is like exploring the universe, the more we understand about it, the more preposterous and mysterious it seems to be.

Anastasia Toufexis tried to help us understand this by exploring the underpinnings of the experience in an article in *Time* magazine some years ago in which she reported on current scientific studies of sex and love.[5] She contended that scientific research, particularly in the fields of biochemistry and anthropology, persuades us that falling in love is a product of central chemical reactions in our bodies, which stimulate the brain with special kinds of secretions. These are dumped into our bloodstreams when we notice special symbolic characteristics of our love object, which turn us on. These secretions of chemicals incite reactions in our central nervous system and create emotional responses that are equivalent to getting high on drugs.

Chemists have been able to identify these chemicals and the specific reactions they cause. They are the components of a combination of forces that generate our feeling of being in love. Toufexis wanted to track down the work of those who apply scientific precision to our understanding of this response process and see whether she could reduce the experience of being in love or falling in love to identifiable chemistry. Her quest was not silly or laughable and her results were well grounded, solid and helpful. She tracked down a number of scientists who were examining these matters and found through their work that falling in love is a complex biological, physiological, and psychological process that is driven by a specific human chemistry. Moreover, it became apparent in her investigation that all aspects of this process are crucial to the long course of human evolution.

"What seems on the surface to be irrational, intoxicated behavior is in fact part of nature's master strategy—a vital force that has helped humans survive, thrive and multiply through thousands of years" (p. 49). She quotes Michael Mills, a psychology professor at Loyola Marymount University in Los Angeles as telling her, "Love is our ancestors whispering in our ears" (p. 49). Being in love, as opposed to simply loving someone in the sense of caring for that person, is grounded solidly on the roots and sources of evolution, mediated through biology and chemistry.

> It was on the plains of Africa about 4 million years ago, in the early days of the human species, that the notion of romantic love probably first began to blossom—or at least that the first cascades of neurochemicals began flowing from the brain to the bloodstream to produce goofy grins and sweaty palms as men and women gazed deeply into each other's eyes. When mankind graduated from scuttling around on all fours to walking on two legs, this change made the whole person visible to fellow human beings for the first time. Sexual organs were in full display, as were other characteristics, from the color of eyes to the span of shoulders. As never before, each individual had a unique allure. (p. 49)

The electric reaction this would have evoked between males and females would have produced new ways of being in love and making love and turning sexual play into a romantic experience, Toufexis suggests. Now being in love could be fun. Sex could be a mode of enjoyment and entertainment, not just of reproduction. Most animals copulate in doggy fashion, but humans can make love face to face. Visual stimuli and the unique attractive qualities of each partner become much more a part of the electricity of the experience. This romanticizing of the experience of falling in love, of being in love, and of cherishing ways of making love may very well have prompted the move toward more careful selectivity in choosing one's lover and the development of longer-term relationships.

Most of us in Western culture have assumed, until recently, that true love lasts long. We still commit ourselves to marriage "until death parts us," and we do not mean the death of the relationship, though we probably should. We mean the death of one of the lovers. However, the experiments on the chemistry of love that Toufexis examined suggest that nature intended love relationships to last about four or five years, just long enough to get a child successfully and safely through infancy. Today we hope the love survives the infancy of a child or the years of child bearing, but most of us recognize that in many folks very substantial changes take place in the dynamics of the relationship because of the refocusing of energy and time on the children.

It has become more unusual than usual for the intense love experience of "being in love" to last for the life of the contract of marriage. A pall of universal sadness reigns in a very large percentage of contractual relationships into which both persons entered some years before, madly in love and with the real belief that their intensity about each other really would last forever. It turns out that one needs to really work at preserving some kind of loving relationship for a sustained number of years, or the love evaporates out of the relationship and people end up just getting used to each other. That is the saddest thing I can imagine anyone saying about a relationship or experiencing in one. Moreover, even if one works hard at preserving the experience of being in love, it is seldom the case that one's partner is as aware of that need or as willing to work at it. Moreover, even under the best circumstances the love makes a transition from the passion of compelling intimacy to the caretaker love of seasoned relationships.

There is a chemical reason for this that has been isolated and described scientifically. In the studies Toufexis reported, 62 cultures were included. In all of them divorce rates peaked after the fourth year of marriage. Children, particularly new young ones, tend to cause the relationship to stay together longer. She says that when a couple has a second child in about three years, their marriage tends to last about four more years. But the relationship then tends to get restless or a bit jaded at about the seventh year. Most of us have seen the movie starring Marilyn Monroe, titled, *The Seven Year Itch.* The reasons for the changes at about the seventh year have to do with the cycle of the chemistry at the root of being in love.

Every human who has had the experience of being swept away by feelings of falling in love is correct about what he or she is feeling. The chemistry of falling in love has to do with the fact that when something in the potential lover triggers the electricity of attraction, our bodies are literally flooded with a very special set of biochemicals. A look, a smile, a smell, a touch, initiates a brain reaction. Or it may be a physical or emotional characteristic, or something infinitely more subtle and unconscious than any of those. That surge of force in the central nervous system releases into the bloodstream large amounts of dopamine, norepinephrine, and phenylethylamine (PEA). These chemicals are very much like amphetamines and have a similar impact when diffused throughout our bodies.

Toufexis tells us that if our physical reaction looks a little like a crisis of stress, it is not surprising because the chemicals and chemical pathways are the same. Experiencing a high state of intoxicated excitement, with flushed face and heavy breathing, is a natural result of the infusion of these chemicals into the bloodstream, and normal to falling in love. Phenylethylamine is the most important chemical in this intense electric event. "But phenylethylamine highs do not last forever, a fact that lends support to arguments that passionate romantic love is short-lived" (p. 50). If someone takes amphetamines his or her body will build up a tolerance to them and one must continue to take larger doses to get the same effect. So it is, also, with PEA. It takes more of it as time goes on, to get as high as the first times. In about three years the body's capacity to produce PEA wears down.

> Fizzling chemicals spell the end of delirious passion; for many people that marks the end of the liaison as well. It is particularly true for those whom Dr. Michael Liebowitz of the New York State Psychiatric Institute terms "attraction junkies." They crave the intoxication of falling in love so much that they move frantically from affair to affair just as soon as the first rush of infatuation fades. (p. 50)

However, there are also reasons that many love relationships last longer than the duration of the body's capacity to produce PEA. As the level of that chemical in the bloodstream declines, the other chemicals mentioned above start to increase. If one still has a lover and works on wholesome congenial relationship, that stimulation increases the production of brain endorphins, which are soothing substances, analgesics, which also provide an increased sense of peace, tranquility, and security. The death of a partner terminates the production of these chemicals and makes one feel horribly "at a loss." With the cherishing partner present the body has a virtually infinite capacity to produce these chemicals for enduring love. The fizz of the PEA may be gone, but the more intimate and sustaining enmeshment with one's lover replaces it and often is even more pleasurable in quite a different way. Toufexis reports that early love is when you love the way the other person makes you feel, but mature love is when you love the person as he or she really is right now.

The brain also produces oxytocin, which prompts females to nuzzle babies and cuddle with their lovers. It probably enhances orgasms by increasing 300 to 400 percent in the bloodstream as one, male or female, works up to climax. So falling in love, being in love, passionate desire to make love, falling out of love, or enduring in love for a lifetime are largely functions of our chemistry. Thank God for such marvelous chemistry! There is, apparently, something divine about it. God created us in God's own image, male and female.

Of course, it is not just our chemistry that connects us. We connect with each other with our whole persons, if we are mature enough to create truly meaningful relationships. However, it is likely to be the case that the insights Toufexis has assembled from a variety of scientific sources explain some of the intense delights and intolerable pains of love relationships. A quarter century ago, Dorothy Tennov published what became a very popular study of human love experiences, in which she tried to get at this matter from the psychological rather than the biochemical perspective.[6] She is a clinical psychologist and became interested in this question because of her own intense experiences of pleasure and pain in falling in and out of love. Much of her own experience is very helpfully reported in her book.

Tennov distinguishes, as her title suggests, between love and limerence. Her definition of the latter seems exactly like the PEA reaction Toufexis found. She speaks of love in ways that seem to correspond to the human experience of a flood of dopamine, norepinephrine, and oxytocin through our circulatory system. Limerence is being in love with love and involves being addicted to the idealized notion of the lover that one has conjured up in one's own mind and heart, prompted by whatever those unconscious buttons of stimulation are that we see in the object of our love and which turn us on. Tennov's study included over 500 people. She actually interviewed

300 persons herself in developing her understanding of this issue. Her book is packed with individual case studies of persons falling in and out of love, described with all the euphoria and excruciating pain that such experience entails. Her definition and elaboration on the meaning of limerence is most helpful:

> To be in a state of limerence is to feel what is usually termed "being in love." It appears that love and sex can coexist without limerence, in fact that any of the three may exist without the others. Human beings are extremely sensitive to each other and easily bruised by rejection or made joyful when given signs of appreciation. When a friendship runs into difficulties, we suffer; when we are able to share our lives with others in the pleasure of what is perceived as mutual understanding and concern, we are strengthened. The person who is not limerent toward you may feel great affection and concern for you, even tenderness, and possibly sexual desire as well. A relationship that includes no limerence may be a far more important one in your life, when all is said and done, than any relationship in which you experienced the strivings of limerent passion. Limerence is not in any way preeminent among types of human attraction or interaction; but when limerence is in full force, it eclipses other relationships. (p. 16)

The unfolding discussion of Tennov's book makes the point that limerence is the source of remarkably delightful experiences for a person, all the more delightful if it is equally experienced by both persons, the lover and the beloved. It is, however, an addictive high that is not quite connected to the mundane realities of everyday life and should, therefore, never be mistaken for true and enduring love. That does not make this scintillating matter of falling in love negative or bad or even to be avoided. It is a gift, like frosting on a cake, when one can experience it with a person who reciprocates and is available for and capable of an enduring relationship of true love. The PEA high is to be sought after but not depended upon to ground good life-shaping decisions or to produce the enduring love of epinephrine and oxytocin. "The relationship between limerence and sex remains extremely complicated" (p. 81). Most of the people she interviewed told Tennov that limerent sex produces the greatest pleasure humans can ever know. However, the evidence of the study tended to the conclusion that the very nature of limerence and of sex itself tend to "conspire to undermine the happiness (long term) except under the luckiest and most extraordinary of circumstances" (p. 81).

Tennov concludes from her study that not only is limerence built into human biology, but it serves a significant purpose in creating a variety of mixtures in the gene pool of the human race, thus enhancing the human community's resilience and potential for survival and creativity. It enhances the necessary fact that, as my grandmother used to say, "There is a pot for every lid—some amazing pots for some amazing lids—out there." The most articulate depiction of the limerent high is presented in Tennov's preface (p. vii). It is worth excerpting here as we move toward the close of this chapter. The limerent person thinks:

> I want you. I want you forever, now, yesterday, and always. Above all, I want you to want me. No matter where I am or what I am doing, I am not safe from your spell. At any moment, the image of your face smiling at me, of your voice telling me you care, or of your hand in mine, may suddenly fill my consciousness, rudely pushing out all else. The expression "thinking of you" fails to convey either the quality or quantity of this unwilled mental activity. "Obsessed" comes closer but leaves out the aching. . . . This pre-possession is an emotional roller-coaster that carries me from the peak of ecstasy to the depths of despair, and back again. I bear the thought of other topics when I must, but prolonged concentration on any other subject is difficult to tolerate. . . . Everything reminds me of you. I try to read, but four times on a single page some word begins the lightning chain of associations that summons my mind away from my work. . . . Often I . . . throw myself upon my bed, and my body lies still while my imagination constructs long and involved and plausible reasons to believe that you love me. . . . After the weekend . . . my brain replayed each moment. Over and over. You said you loved me, at dusk by the waterfall: Ten thousand reverberations of the scene sprinkled my succeeding days with happiness.

Does any one of us not remember such a scene in our own experience? Oh the delicious transcendence! Oh the painful slide down the slippery slope to reality, that is, to more sustaining modes of love and more durable delights of cherishing. The Bible obviously enjoins us to savor and celebrate the delights of the most exotic experiences of love of which we are capable and then calls us to endure in commitment and caring; in cherishing and endearing ourselves to each other in ways that make life long and good and full of grace. God continually calls us, in the Bible, to love each other as he loves us, in terms of the beloved's needs and possibilities, for creativity and joy, by grace-full trust and forgiveness, with nurture and entertainment, out of humor and humility.

Tennov closes her book with the observation that there is a lot of pressure these days to avoid appreciating ourselves as inherently biological creatures. She thinks we need to recapture the humility in which we can face our fundamental natures and shape them to true and honest human and humane values, which come from learning accurately and acknowledging candidly what it means to be human. She has helped us understand what it means to love, to be loved, and to love being in love. Good for her! Good for us!

Whatever it means to be made in the image of God, male and female, it is clear that this business of sex and love is a gift of God, to be savored and celebrated.

Chapter 5

MAKING LOVE: CELEBRATING SEX

Making love is absolutely delightful. Almost everyone who has made love will say so. Most people who have not yet made love but have contemplated it, driven by natural desires to imagine what it will be, already anticipate that it will be a wonderful fulfilling experience. They are right. The Bible implies throughout that sex is a delightful and natural desire and experience. The Bible is for it. It assumes that sexual communion between consenting adults who have a meaningful friendship is a natural, normal, and desirable form of communication and sharing. The Bible enjoins us to enter into such communion with the care and tenderness that holds the personhood of "the other" as a sacred trust.

The Bible does not speak much about sex but it spells out very clearly what sexual behavior is forbidden. It is aggressively against eight kinds of sexual behavior. The eight kinds of forbidden sex are promiscuous sex, incest, pedophilia, necrophilia, bestiality, adultery, homosexual behavior by heterosexual persons, and rape. It almost never mentions all other kinds of sexual behavior and assumes they are being practiced by humankind, universally, and are essential to a life of God's Shalom: peace and prosperity. These would include sexual union within marriage, sexual communion between unmarried consenting adults within a meaningful friendship, and premarital sexuality between persons exploring the possibility of, or engaged in a potential marriage contract.

Jesus spoke positively of sexual union in Matthew 19:5–6 and Mark 10:8 when he said that a husband and wife join in marriage as "one flesh."

Paul is so enthusiastic for the tender sacredness of the "one flesh" union of husbands and wives that he sees it as a symbol of the relationship of Christ and the church, his bride (Eph. 5:21–33). However, the classic passage on the loveliness of making love and celebrating sexuality is, of course, the Song of Songs, also sometimes known as the Song of Solomon. This is an ancient Hebrew poem of striking cadences and remarkably descriptive expostulations about sex. It speaks freely of every sort of healthy exploration of sexual relationship. The special eye-catcher in this exotic erotic poem is the fact that the lovers seem not to be husband and wife. In fact, there seems to be indication in comparing 3:11 with 8:2, 6 that the male in this erotic drama was already married and this is a new lover he has found or who has found him. The beautifully crafted verses suggest that the male "beloved" is King Solomon and that his female "lover" is a "very dark, but comely" and "swarthy" lady. Is it possible that this is an erotic poem about the sexual delights enjoyed by Solomon and the African lady, the Queen of Sheba?

The song opens with the lover longing for her beloved to kiss her profoundly,

> O that you would kiss me
> With the kisses of your mouth,
> For your love is better than wine.

There follows a shower of erotic metaphors in which vineyard, pasture, and nard are euphemisms for the lover's pubic hair, vagina, and vaginal lubrication. The beloved's genitals are "a bag of myrrh" which lies between her breasts, and a bundle of "blooming stalks" which is in her "vineyard." The erotic drama moves with such breathless speed through the cadences of the poem that it is sometimes difficult to keep track of when the lover is gasping out expostulations and when the beloved is rising to gratifying response. He says of her,

> Behold, you are beautiful, my love;
> Behold, you are beautiful;
> Your eyes are doves,
> Behold, you are beautiful, my beloved,
> Truly lovely.

The passion builds, the intensity increases. The lovers are hardly able to get out full sentences. They can not avoid irrationally repeating endearing phrases. Their conscious awareness is moving far from their rational brains deep into their affective psyches. The pitch of passion is increasing. These tendernesses of love are repeated verbatim frequently throughout the song as though they cannot find enough words. The lover sweetly muses:

I am a rose of Sharon
A lily of the valley.

So her beloved responds:

As a lily among brambles,
So is my love among the maidens.

Then she turns even more erotic in her symbolism:

As an apple tree among the trees of the wood,
So is my beloved among young men.
With great delight I sat in his shadow,
And his fruit was sweet to my taste.
He brought me to banqueting
His banner over me was love!

No metaphor seems quite to suffice for her. She looks for more.

My beloved is like a gazelle
Or a young stag.
Our vineyards are in blossom
My beloved pastures his flock among the lilies
Until the day breathes and the shadows flee,
Turn, my beloved, be like a gazelle,
A young stag upon the mountains.

Once again the lover longs for her beloved and this time her longing is unrequited. She cannot find him. She seeks him out and

When I found him whom my soul loves
I held him and would not let him go
Until I had brought him into my house
Into the chamber of conception.

The beloved responds with a soliloquy about the exotic erotic beauty of every square inch of his lover's body. He starts with her hair and eyes, works downward to her teeth and mouth, celebrates her cheeks and neck, and nearly gets grounded out or preoccupied with her two fawnlike breasts.

For some time he forgets to go on. But then he remembers that there is more of her further down this wonderful litany of love. He reminds himself:

> I will hie me to the mountain of myrrh
> And the hill of frankincense.
> You are all fair, my love;
> There is no flaw in you.

Then the beloved spends a lot of time down there at the mound of Venus:

> You have ravished my heart,
> You have ravished my heart,
> How sweet is your love.
> Better your love than wine
> The fragrance of your oil than spice.
> Your lips distill nectar.

He tells her she smells better than a pine forest, her juices are tastier than milk and honey. The lips of her vulva amaze him. She is like a garden of choicest fruits, and her scent is a combination of nard and saffron, calamus and cinnamon, incense and myrrh, aloes and all the most sought-after spices. From her mound of Venus her love juices are like a garden fountain, a well of living water, and a flowing stream from the mountains of Lebanon. His lover responds by inviting him to

> Blow upon my garden,
> Let its fragrance be wafted abroad.
> Let my beloved come into his garden
> And eat its choicest fruits.

He answers:

> I come to my garden, my bride.
> I gather my myrrh with my spice.
> I eat my honeycomb with my honey.
> I drink my wine with my milk.
> Open to me my love, my dove, my perfect one.

The lover lets us in on her excitement:

> I had put off my garment,
> How could I put it on!

My beloved put his hand to my latch
And my heart was thrilled within me!

There follows her litany of celebration of every square inch of his body, from his ruddy radiant complexion, to his black hair, his eyes, cheeks, lips, arms, his body like ivory work, his legs like alabaster columns, his speech most sweet. In fact, she concludes, seemingly running out of adequate words,

He is altogether desirable.
This is my beloved, my friend.
I am my beloved's and my beloved is mine.

The final three chapters of the Song of Solomon are a crescendo of competing litanies in which the lover and beloved try to outdo each other in their list of symbols and metaphors for describing every iota of beauty in the entire body of the other. Finally, it all comes to a climax and finale, when the lover cries out for another round of passionate intercourse:

Make haste, my beloved,
And be like a gazelle
A young stag
Upon the mountain of spices.

Well, anyone who has ever made love or imagined making love with a lovely lover or beloved, would certainly like a sexual romp like that biblical one! We clearly have here the Bible's model that sets forth the ideal joy of sex, as a gift of God and an experience both normal and wholesome for humankind.

It is humorous to the point of hilarity how the interpreters of the Song of Songs have tried to handle this richly erotic embroidery of sensual symbolism over the centuries. One can imagine the exciting and extensive debate about whether this book should be a part of the Bible that must have unfolded at the Council of Rabbis who met at Jamnia in 90 C.E. They gathered to determine which books should be part of the *Hebrew Bible.* Of course, generally speaking, the Jewish leaders of that time as well as the rabbis who established Judaism as we know it today, during the period of 300–600 C.E., tended to be rather humane and earthy realists. They would, in the main, have seen this song for what it really is and intends to be. There was the occasional voice that claimed it was too erotic to be in the Bible and too sensual to be taken literally. Such folk attempted to turn the entire song into a metaphor for God's love relationship with his special people.

Initially, the Christian community seems to have had no difficulty in seeing the Song of Songs for what it is, a delightfully erotic celebration of one of God's great gifts to his created world: sex. At the Council of Nicea, in 325 C.E., when the Christian bishops met to determine, among other things, what should be the contents of the Christian Scriptures, they did not hesitate to take the Jamnia decision at face value for the OT, and moved on smartly to consider what should constitute the NT. Apparently, they had no great difficulty with the Song of Songs.

However, after the influence of St. Jerome and St. Augustine started to permeate the church slightly more than a half-century after Nicea, Christians began to denigrate sex, idealize celibacy, and call into question the meaning of the Song of Songs. Their problem was that it was in the Bible and had always been in the Bible. But it was either blatantly erotic, an uncomely thing for a holy book, or it must be a metaphor. It did not take long for the bishops who were, in any case moving increasingly toward celibacy as the standard for clergy, to adopt the option that this erotic poem was a spiritualized metaphor. So the tradition was solidly established throughout Christendom by the sixth or seventh century that the Song of Songs was really about God's love for the church and the church's love for God. Few seemed to see the inherent humor in trying to read Christ's relationship to the church in terms of the graphic moves described in the song. Does Christ really do something like that to the church and does the church really feel like that about Christ?

This way of looking at things was quickly tied to Paul's remark in Ephesians 5:21–32, in which he declares that the relationship between husband and wife is an analogy drawn from the analogue of the relation of Christ and the church.

> The husband is the head of the wife as Christ is the head of the church, his body, and is himself its Savior. . . . Husbands love your wives, as Christ loved the church and gave himself up for her. . . . For no man ever hates his own flesh, but nourishes it and cherishes it, as Christ does the church, because we are members of his body. For this reason a man shall leave his father and mother and be joined to his wife, and the two shall become one. This is a great mystery, and I take it to mean Christ and the church.

Moreover, the Gospel of John and the Revelation of St. John both refer rather frequently to the church as the bride of Christ.[1]

There are a number of reasons why this is a downright hilarious interpretation of the Song of Songs. First, it is quite obvious that the song intends to be exactly what it is, namely an uproariously successful erotic celebration of robust sexual play. Second, the song is wholly unapologetic of its exotic erotic quality because the author is sure that such sexual delight is what God intended and it should be publicly celebrated by godly people. Third, the religious authorities who made the decision to include it in the *Hebrew Bible* were clearly and consciously on this same wavelength. Fourth, the Christian bishops who agreed with those Hebrew religious authorities by adopting the whole *Hebrew Bible* into the Christian Scriptures and calling it the *Holy Bible* obviously also agreed with their rationale and that of the author of the Song of Songs.

Fifth, the Christian embarrassment and shame over the delightfully erotic qualities, cadences, and crescendos of the Song of Songs developed after Jerome's embarrassing sexual misadventures and Augustine's riotously licentious youthful life; and it developed under the sexually negative influence of these two overreacting sensualistic theologians upon the thought forms of the later church. Sixth, the church has followed that influence for 17 centuries like a dumb ox deprived of its fodder but seeking no new pasture. Seventh, the unbiblical factor in all this is the perspective of the church, too embarrassed by the literal sensuality of the Song of Songs to admit its wonderful God-given truths. The literal celebration of rich robust sex and sensuality is not unbiblical! What a hilarious joke that it was ever thought to be so.

Fortunately, as in the case of most things bishops, pastors, and theologians say, the constituency of the church throughout the centuries did not pay much attention to this denigration of sex and the Song of Songs, at least so far as its behavior was concerned. However, the stupid attitude of the official church on this issue throughout history, did, unfortunately, keep the people of God in a mind-set of ambiguity about really enjoying sexuality unabashedly as God obviously intended. Those damnable bishops spoiled a lot of godly fun and wholesome pleasure by inducing false shame and guilt, and the fear usually attached to those useless emotions.

Moreover, as is always the case with erroneously repressed emotions, the longings sprang up in naughty alternative behavior. The bishops' emphasis upon sex for procreation only, probably had more than any other factor to do with the repression of wholesome joyful lovemaking and the resort instead to destructive searches for merely having illicit or promiscuous sex. The corporate church owes the world of humans an enormous apology for the centuries-long lie it perpetrated in this regard, and for the psychological and social pathology it produced.

There are, of course, other passages in Scripture in which robust erotic exploration is approved, indeed encouraged. The Book of Ruth is a story of love. The dynamics of love run in various directions in that narrative. Elimelech and Naomi have two sons, Mahlon and Chilion, who fall in love, respectively, with Orpah and Ruth. Eventually all the men die, leaving the three women. Orpah returns to her father's house but Ruth devotes herself to Naomi. Soon she becomes acquainted with Boaz, a relative of Naomi with whom both women think she should try to become married. Naomi instructs Ruth on how to find Boaz in his bed and seduce him sexually, a project she accepts readily, proceeds with immediately, and carries out with the great skill and success of a professional. Nowhere in the Bible is this delightful story judged negatively. Indeed, Ruth is forever after celebrated as one of the key ancestors of the Messiah, seen by Christians to be Jesus Christ.

Similarly, when the Israelite spies were sent to spy out the land of Canaan in preparation for Israel's invasion under Joshua, they stopped in at the home of Rahab, a professional prostitute (Joshua 2). It is clear from the biblical story that Rahab took care of the spies, gave them good information about the city of Jericho, and sent them on their way. When the invasion of Canaan came, Rahab was spared because of her care for the spies, and she too became a celebrated ancestor of the Messiah.

Esther is, perhaps, the most colorful sexual player of all in the *Hebrew Bible*. Her story is told in the biblical Book of Esther. Esther lived in the land of Persia (485–465 B.C.E.) with the Israelites who carried there into exile. Her beauty brought her to the attention of the king of Persia and he acquired her for his harem. When destructive forces within the empire undertook to destroy the Jews, she went to the king, sexually seduced him, and persuaded him thereby to hang the perpetrators and protect the Jews. She is celebrated to this day as a deliverer of her people. The annual Jewish festival of Purim is a commemoration of her courage and skill.

The celebrated roles of Ruth, Rahab, and Esther all point to women who employed the power of their sexuality to achieve important objectives. They stand in contrast to Tamar, who was a widow of Judah's son (Genesis 38). She was promised in marriage to Judah's surviving son, as Israelite law demanded, but he never got around to setting up the wedding. Tamar heard Judah was coming through her town to shear his sheep and set herself up as a prostitute on the road. Judah noticed the attractive but veiled prostitute and made love to her. In the process she demanded a surety of him and he gave her his ring and staff. She became pregnant so she informed him and sent him the surety he had given her. He said, "She was more righteous than I" and, of course, he cared for her from then on. The interesting aspects of this story are not Tamar's promiscuity but, first, the fact that in her completely unempowered state she successfully used her sexuality to get justice, the justice that had been due her under the law, long since. Second, the Bible nowhere judges Tamar negatively or suggests that her sexual play was inappropriate, immoral, unnatural, or sinful. It just is.

By the way, she had twins; lovely, healthy Perez and Zerah. Good guys. The Bible does not overmoralize sex! Unfortunately, some Bible interpreters do. That is obscene, as abuse of the truth always is.

Chapter 6

MAKING BABIES: PURPOSES OF SEX

So it is clear from the Song of Songs that the joy of sex, the delights of making love, the celebration of sensual playfulness, and the union of sexual intercourse are all important purposes of human sexuality. However, there is a story in the *Hebrew Bible* that called this into question at a very early stage of the development of the Bible as Sacred Scripture. The story is about Onan, the son of Judah and grandson of Jacob, the Patriarch. It is a small story, a completely irrelevant story these days, but a story that did a lot of damage over the centuries. The story appears in Genesis 38:7–10, in the middle of the report about Judah and Tamar, which we have already discussed. Notice what the Bible says.

> Er, Judah's first-born, was wicked in the sight of the Lord; and the Lord slew him. Then Judah said to Onan, "Go in to your brother's wife, and perform the duty of a brother-in-law to her, and raise up offspring for your brother." But Onan knew that the offspring would not be his; so when he went in to his brother's wife he spilled the semen on the ground, lest he should give offspring to his brother. And what he did was displeasing in the sight of the Lord, and he slew him also.

This narrative is about the required behavior within the patriarchal family under an ancient law of Near Eastern culture. The law probably originated in ancient Egyptian or Babylonian legal codes. Its purpose was clear, readily understandable, and wise in the setting of those ancient cultures. It was designed (1) to preserve the name of a man who died young without progeny or heir, (2) to provide a clear line of legal inheritance of the estate of the dead man, and (3) to ensure that his widow had family to care for her in her advancing years. It required that a woman, who was left as a widow without children upon the death of her husband, should be taken to wife by her husband's brother. He was required to give her children who would be raised as the children and heirs of his dead brother. The law was incorporated into early Israelite social regulation.

> If brothers dwell together, and one of them dies and has no son, the wife of the dead shall not be married outside the family to a stranger; her husband's brother shall go in to her, and take her as his wife, and perform the duty of a husband's brother to her. And the first son whom she bears shall succeed to the name of his brother who is dead, that his name may not be blotted out of Israel. (Deuteronomy 25:5–6)

It was to this regulation that the funny story about Jesus' chat with the Sadducees referred. The Sadducees addressed Jesus with the enigma of the man who died, leaving a childless widow (Mark 12:18–27). In keeping with the instructions of Moses' law, the man's brother took her to wife but died also leaving her childless. So it went down the line of seven brothers. All married her in keeping with the law and all left her childless. So the Sadducees challenged Jesus as to whose wife she would be in the resurrection. They had two objectives. First, they did not believe in any resurrection and they knew Jesus did. Second, they thought they had him on the technical point of the Mosaic Torah. If he really thought there would be a resurrection, how could he sort out the enigma of this apparently very durable lady and the seven brothers that she had apparently completely worn out.

Jesus' response is a neat joke. He said, "Well, on the point of resurrection, Moses' writings tell us that God is the God of Abraham, Isaac, and Jacob. Obviously, he is the God of the living, not of the dead. So those ancient patriarchs must be resurrected and enjoying eternal life. Moreover, on the point of whose wife she is to be in eternity, your notion is really off base. In heaven there will be neither marriage relationships nor marriage ceremonies." Jesus' implication was that she would be the partner of all seven brothers. Obviously, Jesus was clear on the fact that heaven is a setting of holy promiscuity, where we shall enjoy total union with everyone who really delights us. Why not, of course, since presumably in our glorified bodies (1 Corinthians 15) and whole and complete spirits, there will be no such thing as jealousy or obstructive or negative emotions.

Surely this humorful response of Jesus to the Sadducees, in which he overwhelmingly turned the flank of their specious argument, is related to his other remark to those who wished to stump him with the question about divorce (Matthew 5:28). He did not forbid divorce in every case, but said that it is generally a bad idea because even adultery can be forgiven just like any other sin, since it is no worse than lust. All humans look upon persons of the opposite sex and lust after them, "committing adultery with them already in their hearts." It is an ordinary, everyday, human experience, which can neither be helped nor prevented, and need not be prevented. It can readily be forgiven, as can adultery, according to Jesus.

The law to which Judah appealed when his eldest son, Er, died young, leaving his widow, Tamar, childless, was a guarantee of good social order. Nothing put a woman into a more vulnerable and pitiable status and condition in the ancient Near East than being left as a widow. Her circumstance was particularly unfortunate if she were a young widow with neither money nor offspring. She was vulnerable to the predatory abuses of the males who knew of her condition and was often left with little alternative choice than prostitution, to make a meager subsistence living. The only thing worse than a young widow, in that time and culture, was a young orphan, particularly a young female orphan. Therefore, we have the injunction throughout the Bible that we must always look after the widows and orphans. Thus the first appointment of church officers in the NT was to provide deacons to look after the widows (Acts 6:1–6).

The *Hebrew Bible* law that a brother should take to wife a dead man's childless widow provided a guarantee that she would not become a castoff of society but would be incorporated into a wholesome family, the family in which she had been established before her husband died. Presumably, this would inevitably be a family in which she was loved and cherished in her own right and for the memory of her dead husband, in this case, the eldest son in the patriarchal family of Judah. Moreover, this (1) provided for the social welfare of the widow and of her subsequently conceived children, (2) ensured her economic viability, (3) guaranteed her sexual and emotional fulfillment, and (4) preserved both her own good name and that of her dead husband. Her children, conceived by her dead husband's brother, provided a genetically coherent line of heirs to her original husband and took his name as theirs.

The entire arrangement was a really good setup, in many ways a lot better provision for well-being than the kind of social welfare programs we have in our *sophisticated* modern societies today. This provision for the care of widows, and preservation of both the genetic lines and genealogical memories within extended families, was really ingenious; and it prevailed for many centuries because it was so relevant to the cultures and societies of the ancient Near East. Basically, it was a side effect of or corollary to the social welfare practices that produced polygamy in those ancient societies.

Now the problem in the story of Onan is that he accepts the responsibility to provide his brother's wife social security and sexual fulfillment, but he refuses to provide progeny or an heir for his brother. No reason is given for this diffidence to the spirit of the law on Onan's part, while he exercised the letter of the law, at least so far as the family could discern. That is, he had intercourse with his brother's wife but he intentionally "spilled his semen on the ground" to prevent her getting pregnant by him. He practiced coitus interruptus whenever he made love to Tamar.

We may have a clue to his reasons for refusing to get Tamar pregnant, in an early line in the larger narrative about Judah, Tamar, and her dead husband, Er. The story tells us that Er was a wicked fellow in the sight of the Lord. That is why he was dead. Perhaps Onan hated him for his wickedness and refused to perpetuate his name in Onan's own progeny, who would be dedicated to the memory of his dead brother, Er. One could understand that sort of anguish in the man, and his hesitancy—even refusal. Why preserve the memory of such a wicked and tragic man? We can sympathize with Onan. Unfortunately, God did not sympathize with him, at least that is how the story goes. God killed him for coitus interruptus. Capital offense?

Of course, we should not push this notion of Onan's reasons too far, because we surely cannot take very seriously the claim that Er's death was caused by his wickedness in the sight of the Lord. Any Lord God who would be so displeased by Onan's coitus interruptus that he would kill him for it cannot be taken seriously in claiming that Er was wicked and so God killed him. Such a God should, himself, be exterminated. Er was probably a rather nice guy, as was Onan, apart from his selfishness in refusing to raise up children to his brother. So we may need to look in other directions for Onan's reasons for not wanting to do that. Perhaps he had 15 children and his brother left no estate, so he was unclear on how he could support more kids. That would be understandable.

Perhaps Onan sensed that Tamar was a domineering and manipulative female who had some hand in his brother's death. She certainly proved to be enormously deceptive, manipulative, self-centered, and controlling in her enticement and seduction of Judah a little later. There was something about her that put people off, particularly people from her husband's family. They knew something about her that we are not told. The data for that is simple and can be extrapolated from the story. First, when her husband,

Er, died, she did not stay in his family, as was the usual case, but they sent her to her father's house. Second, when Judah instructed Onan to take her to wife, he basically refused to perform the legal requirement. Third, when she knew Judah was coming through her town, she set herself up as a prostitute and ensnared him. Fourth, to control the situation and teach him a lesson for not giving her his third son in marriage as the law required, she required of him his ring and staff until he could pay her in kind for the lovemaking. Fifth, when he could not find her to pay her, she revealed to him that she was pregnant. Sixth, we have no assurance except her claim that she was pregnant by Judah. Seventh, Judah agreed to look after her but did not take her to wife, as he could have done.

There was something about her that put men off. Maybe Onan was not so dumb after all. Did he know something about her that he judged made her a lousy wife and a bad mother who would be obsessively controlling of her husband, and worse, of her children? He would not give her children (38:9). Judah could have given her children, either himself, or by his third son; but he did not, at least he did not until she tricked him into it, and then he refused to give her any more. "He did not lie with her again" (38:26).

Well, it is the weight of that really crazy report in Genesis 38:9–10 that has caused this ridiculous story to do so much damage in society over the years. First of all, for centuries it caused Jews and Christians to use this scripture as an argument to turn the very natural experience of masturbation into an evil behavior, even a terrifying sin against God. The Roman Catholic Church, throughout its history and even today, contends officially that sexual behavior is primarily for reproduction and that any sexual act that is used in any other way is a sin against God's will and God's design for humans. Thus, semen is a sacred fluid which has within it the potential for human life and so, if it is intentionally wasted or misused, that is a serious immoral and unethical act, according to Catholic dogma and practice. This line of reasoning has also been extended to the female contribution to human life, namely, the pre-embryonic egg that a woman produces.

So the judgment the Bible delivers upon Onan in Genesis 38:10 is extrapolated to mean that masturbation on the part of the human male is a capital offense in the sight of God. This gave rise to the frequent admonition many young Catholic boys were given, namely, that if they masturbated they would go blind. Such terrifying imagery about masturbation, and similar lies about other kinds of sexual behavior, did quite amazing destruction to the normal healthy sexual function of many young Catholic men.

Moreover, taking this story of Onan literally and giving it the meaning that his sin was his destruction of his life-bearing seed, by wasting it on the ground, led the Roman Catholic Church to its absurd and enormously destructive present-day theology of birth control. The rationale of this theology starts with the assumption that the wasting of any semen or egg is an offense against God, who is the God of life; because it destroys the God-given potential for life. The next assumption is that only God can decide upon the promotion or destruction of life. The following step in this line of argument is that sex is for reproduction. Humans are called by God to copulate. Only God can decide whether a given copulation will produce an offspring. Humans may not manipulate this process or in any way obstruct reproduction. Therefore, birth control of any kind is against God's will and law.

This official decree has resulted in many lovely large Catholic families, and many popular humorful stories. When I was an Army Chaplain in the 8th Infantry Division, I was 28 years old and had five children. In my day that was considered a large family. I had never thought of it that way because my father was one of 15 siblings, my mother one of 9, and I one of 9. However, when I was transferred from the division assignment to the Landstuhl Army Medical Center, someone who heard of the young chaplain arriving with his five children remarked, "Gee, he must be a Catholic Chaplain." When I arrived, I set them straight by saying, "No. I am just a sexy Protestant." Mary Jo and I decided to have the children close together while I was on active army duty because Uncle Sam paid for them all. They cost me $11.00 each at that time. Good family planning!

Unfortunately, the Onan-based sexual and social doctrine of the Roman Catholic Church, shared by most Protestant churches until quite recently, has had less than humorous societal results. Not only have many people been perplexed and ambivalent about their own sexuality and sexual freedom because of such codes as just described regarding masturbation and birth control; but the destructive consequences have pervaded all of Western culture and become worldwide in their wretched effects. This is all the more tragic in view of the fact that the entire perspective on sexuality is based upon a completely unbiblical interpretation of the story of Onan.

First of all, the law requiring a brother to take his dead brother's widow to wife and raise children to him no longer applies, any more than the regulations in favor of polygamy in ancient societies apply to our day and its social order. Even in the setting of the ancient patriarchs, when the law did apply, the reason Onan was found in breach of that ancient Mosaic regulation was not because he wasted his semen and thereby killed off the potential for its life-giving future. His error was that he refused to perpetuate the memory, name, and lineage of his brother; and in so doing, he refused to provide the life-fulfillment and security, namely progeny, for his brother's widow that the law required.

So the unbiblical Roman Catholic theology of masturbation and birth control has resulted in the fact that the church has viewed birth control and abortion as equivalent. This monolithic outlook prevented the church at and after Vatican II to follow the implications of Pope John XXIII's new and biblical initiatives to see abortion as one thing and birth control as something quite different. Had it not been for this strange story of Onan, misinterpreted by the church's theologians for centuries as forbidding the destructions of unfertilized eggs and sperm, the Roman Catholic Church could have led the world into a wise and wholesome course of action that could have approved and encouraged preconception birth control and forbidden abortion. The world would have seen that posture, almost certainly, as the moral high ground, and followed it in the main. Certainly Christendom would have stood unified on that issue, I believe. That would have prevented the intentional abortion of many of the 80 million unborn American children intentionally aborted and destroyed during the last 40 years, to say nothing of the statistics for the rest of the world. How tragic it is to think that in some direct or indirect way the Christian Church might be thought to have the blood of these aborted children on its hands!

Of course, it is the case that one of the emphases of the Bible regarding human sexuality is upon the importance of reproduction and perpetuation of the human race. Already in the very first chapter of the Bible we have God's imperative that we reproduce.

> God created humankind in his own image, in the image of God he created them, male and female he created them. And God blessed them, and God said to them, "Be fruitful and multiply, and fill the earth and subdue it; and have dominion over the fish of the sea and over the birds of the air and over every living thing that moves upon the earth." (Genesis 1:27–28)

I, personally, take this cultural mandate seriously. However, I see it as meaning that we are called by God to facilitate the created world in doing its very best to fulfill all its enormous God-given potential and express fully the entire range of possibilities with which God has invested it in its evolutionary creation.

That means, of course, that we must perpetuate the human race, that we must multiply it responsibly, and that we must create such an aesthetic culture of science and thought as reflects the beauty and imagination of God's mind and spirit; the mind and spirit that he has invested and incarnated in our minds and spirits. It means also that we must exploit the resources of this universe so as to infinitely advance our knowledge and enhance our creativity, thinking God's thoughts after him and doing God's work in God's name. A significant part of that creating after the image of God is the fashioning of a free and joyful sexual existence as God's human beings. This notion of being fruitful and multiplying and replenishing the earth is not only an instruction given at the outset of the biblical story. It is a notion that is reinforced repeatedly throughout the entire Bible.

However, the Bible nowhere suggests that reproduction is the primary purpose of sexuality. There is clear indication, as we noted in chapter 5, that the celebration of sexuality in itself is an equally important human endeavor and objective in life. The joy of sex is as important a biblically enjoined purpose as is reproduction. Making love is as important to God as is making babies. Making love as a mode of human communication and a method of exploring each other's persons and personalities is an essentially biblical theme, leading to the biblical notion that two humans by sexual play become "one flesh," a notion found in the OT, in Jesus' words, and in St. Paul's epistles. This "one flesh" idea means that sex can bring about a profound connection at the deepest visceral level. Only in sexual union and in spiritual communion do we reach that profound, wholesome, and holy enmeshment.

Chapter 7

SIN AND SEDUCTION: ADAM, EVE, AND SEX PROBLEMS

There are two graphic stories in the Bible about how evil entered into this world, and both of them are about sex and seduction. Most readers of the Bible are completely unaware that there are two such stories and that they are both about sexual manipulation and abuse. There are quite a number of stories in the Bible about sex and seduction, and in some of the narratives such behavior is described as bad behavior. It is surprising from our modern point of view that the Bible does not, in every one of those cases, call attention to this behavior as sinful or evil. In the cases of Ruth, Esther, Rahab, and Jael (Judges 4), for example, their sexual seductions are said to produce important results in God's scheme of things.

The first of the two stories about how evil entered our human world is found in Genesis 3:1–24 and the second one in Genesis 6:1–8. In other words, they are both in the very first book of the Bible and in the founding myths of the ancient Israelites' view of the world and of life before the face of God. Most Bible students are quite familiar with the narrative in Genesis 3, but few have noticed, with any meaningful degree of attention, the import of the story in Genesis 6. If they have noticed it, they have had no good idea what to make of it. Our thinking about how evil, pain, and grief entered human experience is dominated by the story in Genesis 3.

It is of great interest, of course, that the ancient Bible authors associated sexuality with the fall of humans from a pristine state into sin, suffering, death. Indeed, they connected this entrance of grief and abuse into the world specifically with sex and seduction. Moreover, the seduction in both narratives takes the form of enticement rather than force or rape. In the end, the stories are about informed adult consent to a manipulative process leading to intercourse: social and sexual.

The second narrative was in fact the first one to appear in Israelite religious literature as an explanation of how things in this world ran amuck in suffering and conflict. That story of illicit sexual relationships between the sons of God and the daughters of men was for many centuries the main Israelite explanation for sin and evil in this world. This was the Israelite view of things long before the story of Adam and Eve and the serpent replaced it. The story in Genesis 6 is brief, simple, and tight-lipped, so to speak.

> When men began to multiply on the face of the ground and daughters were born to them, the sons of God saw that the daughters of men were fair; and they took to wife such of them as they chose. Then the Lord said, "My spirit shall not abide in man for ever, for he is flesh, but his days shall be a hundred and twenty years." The Nephilim were on the earth in those days, and also afterward, when the sons of God came in to the daughters of men, and they bore children to them. These were the mighty men that were of old, the men of renown. The Lord saw that the wickedness of man was great in the earth, and that every imagination of the thoughts of his heart was only evil continually. And the Lord was sorry that he had made man on the earth, and it grieved him to his heart. (1–6)

This telling of the story is so cryptic as to leave one wondering why God was so disturbed by the sexual behavior described. Moreover, the line between the sexual behavior and the rise of suffering and evil is not clear in this account. In fact, the way the story is told here is ambivalent about the rise of evil in the world of humans. Whereas it implies that God was displeased by the sexual behavior of the "sons of God," the story suggests that "mighty men of renown" were the product of this miscegenation between heavenly males and earthly females. Nonetheless, until the centuries immediately before the time of Christ, this was the story by which most Israelites explained the problem of sin and evil. The reason for that seems to lie in the fact that an earlier and much more elaborate form of this story is contained in an ancient Israelite book called the Book of the Watchers, later incorporated into 1 Enoch, an apocryphal book.

1 Enoch seems to have had great influence upon Jews during the centuries just before Jesus. In the Book of the Watchers the sexual behavior of the angels, referred to as the sons of God in Genesis 6, is severely condemned by God and punished. From this story comes the tradition of the fallen angels that we have in Judaism and Christianity, so lyrically

celebrated in John Milton's *Paradise Lost* and *Paradise Regained.*[1] Today scholars debate vigorously what it was about the sons of God taking human females as wives that was so evil and was supposed to have caused such evil consequences. Some contend that it taught humans to be sexual. Others that it was a violation of boundaries, not sexual boundaries so much as the boundary between the heavenly realm and the earthly realm. Still others suggest that the angels taught humans the fashioning and use of weapons, introducing technology-enhanced violence on earth.

In the end it makes little difference which was intended by the story. The case is that the Israelites believed for 1,000 years or so that this story about sex and seduction explained the origin of pain and evil as something that fallen angels brought from heaven into the human world. This story was eclipsed and replaced, as the main narrative about the origin of evil, by the fall story in Genesis 3. This eclipse took place soon after the Babylonian Exile and under the influence of stories that the Israelites found in ancient Mesopotamian religious lore. This story in Genesis 3 explains pain and evil as having been generated within the human world by human disobedience to God.

The fall story in Genesis 3 is a rewrite, of course, of a much more ancient Mesopotamian fertility story of sex and seduction.[2] Genesis 3 is a theological myth in the form of a dramatic narrative of extraordinary literary quality, which attempts to take account of the incongruity between the righteousness of God and the problem of pain in God's created universe. It was edited by an Israelite theologian to make the Genesis account fit the essential requirements of an early Hebrew religious worldview, in which the Israelite God, Yahweh Elohim, is the divine character and Adam and Eve are the representatives of the whole human race. To appreciate its full weight the passage must be read through both a religious and psychological lens. We will try to do that here in order to see how this old story attempts to explain the manner in which humankind fell into pain, perplexity, and alienation.

So in the Bible this Mesopotamian story was rewritten to make it a story about Yahweh, the God of the Bible, and his relationship with the world and humans. In this narrative we have a double seduction. The serpent seduced Eve, the virgin. Eve seduced Adam by explaining to him his potential for "acquiring fruit." When he was "taken in" by her, both of them realized that they had (1) learned an entirely new world of reality, (2) become very self-conscious of their physical selves and their sexual polarity, and (3) learned to feel shamed because they were anxious about this new unknown world and separated from their childlike naiveté. They now knew each other, from the inside out; and they knew themselves as never before. The "fall" is really a "rise," a maturation, an awakening to new possibilities that are both pleasurable and painful. They came to know "both good and evil."[3]

> The Lord God commanded the man, saying, "You may freely eat of every tree of the garden, but of the tree of knowledge of good and evil you shall not eat, for in the day that you eat of it you shall die." . . . Adam and his wife were both naked, and were not ashamed. Now the serpent . . . said to the woman, "Did God say, 'You shall not eat of any tree of the garden'?" And the woman said to the serpent, "We may eat of the fruit of the trees of the garden; but God said, 'You shall not eat of the fruit of the tree which is in the midst of the garden . . . lest you die.'" But the serpent said to the woman, "You will not die. For God knows that when you eat of it your eyes will be opened, and you will be like God, knowing good and evil." . . . So when the woman saw . . . that the tree was to be desired to make one wise, she took of its fruit and ate; and she also gave some to her husband, and he ate. Then the eyes of both were opened, and they knew that they were naked. . . . Then the Lord God said . . . "I will greatly multiply your pain. . . ." (Genesis 2:16–3:16a)

Incidentally, the serpent is not here intended to be Satan but rather an admired and "most subtle" animal in God's garden. That serpent was a phallic symbol in the Mesopotamian fertility myths. The fruiting trees in the story are also fertility symbols. Adam and Eve have moved from the nursery into the adolescent awareness of postpubescence. The psychology and spirituality of this story of seduction and maturation is intriguing for our understanding of all the biblical narratives about sexuality.

Whether it is understood literally, metaphorically, mythically, or symbolically, we all recognize immediately the authenticity of this story as an accurate comment upon the problem of pain. All healthy humans, at the center of our psyches, feel a certain incompleteness and loneliness. We long for more meaning in our hunger for each other and for God. Moreover, we automatically, with the naiveté of children, tend to internalize this loneliness and anxiety in a sense of shame or guilt. We feel that there must be something wrong with us, since we feel such incompleteness in ourselves and feelings of being so out of touch with others and with God.

Genesis 2:25–3:24 is one of those stories that carries with it such deep psychological quality that we sense at once that it touches, at the center, an obvious truth of human history and vital personal experience. Of course, the story is mythic and not about historical events. The narrative speaks of the radical and tragic distance we experience between the perfect world we can imagine and the flawed world we create. That distance we call pain and evil. It is amazing that the ancient Hebrews thought that was caused by seduction: sexual and psychological.

Though the story is not explicitly sexual, it is the story of a contest between two potential lovers, God and the serpent, struggling for the allegiance of a virgin. As we have already noted, it is the story of a double seduction (serpent-Eve, Eve-Adam) and of the very human response of guilt. It is also a story of the sense of shame and anxiety surrounding sexual awareness, vulnerability, and exploitation. Moreover, it is a story about the anxiety that arises in us when we become conscious of our power over our own destiny and of our potential for achieving ultimate meaning and ultimate self-destruction. Adam and Eve's eyes were opened and they knew good and evil, and they lost their Paradise. The story is equally intriguing for the manner in which the Hebrew editors attempted to adapt it to their religious outlook and thereby reveal something essential about the manner in which God relates to the impaired universe and to the fractured human community of sexual and seductive persons. God is disappointed, the text says.

Whether we take this text literally or metaphorically, it is clear that the ancient editor intended the story to describe the character of God as a sovereign ruler, the nature of humans as flawed, the nature of the universe as malignant, and the predicament of humans as that of willful persons caught in a world in which human action produces the kind of divine reaction that spells important consequences for humans, for good or ill. This outlook has four crucial implications: God is arbitrary. The problem of evil is a human problem within the created world, and not a heavenly problem as in the case of the story in Genesis 6. God is not accountable for the fact that humans can and will make self-destructive choices. The central problem of human self-defeat is seduction and that is mainly related to human sexuality.

For centuries Jews and Christians have wrestled with the big problems in that ancient Jewish editor's ideas. Did a good God create a flawed creation with a potential for human evil? How can an ethereal God of ineffable pure spirit be related to a malignant material universe? Is it really true that humans, with limited human knowledge, are held ultimately accountable for our very human mistakes? Since we are commissioned in Genesis 1:28 to act creatively in our world, with a limited data base, how can God be so disturbed by the flaws in our experiment? What happens to God's integrity, in Genesis 3, when there is such poor proportionality between human motives and actions, on the one hand, and the massive painful consequences

God wreaks upon the entire universe because of them, on the other hand? The punishment does not fit the crime. Even we, flawed humans, know better than to behave so brutally as God does in that story.

So the story served the *Hebrew Bible* readers by providing them with a description of the psychological and spiritual state of affairs they thought afflicted humans. They saw themselves and the human race as alienated, orphaned, and diseased; and they were, of course, correct. Moreover, they connected this condition with the vulnerability and ambivalence they felt about sex. That set the course for centuries of Bible believers feeling ambivalent and troubled about sexuality, because they believed this story indicated that God had a negative view of human sexual play. So humans have erroneously, but persistently, associated sex with guilt and shame. It is particularly tragic that so much mayhem could be wreaked for centuries upon human sexuality because of a lousy story imported into biblical literature from a pagan Mesopotamian source.

A variety of psychological perspectives may be employed to understand the elements and the significance of all that. The symbols in the story are telling: fertility symbols (virgin and fruit trees), phallic symbols (serpent and flaming sword), vulnerability symbols (nakedness, anxiety, and shame), a phallic deity (powerful) and nonphallic humans (dependent). In a Freudian model this narrative describes the generalized state of neurotic anxiety humans experience about our identity, generativity, individuation, phallic assertiveness, and mortality. This neurosis is an expression of the dissonance we feel between our super-ego as introjected divine authority; our id as the authentic phallic force of individuation, assertiveness, and independence; and our ego, which endeavors to work out a successful operational settlement between the two.

In this Freudian model, Genesis 3 is a symbolic description of the primal dynamics of human maturation and of the inevitably complex and potentially tragic process of trying to establish a discrete and affirmable self. A Jungian lens for reading the passage would likely bring into central focus an even more archetypal reading of the symbolic elements in the narrative, concentrating upon the masculine authority of Yahweh, the womblike qualities of Eden, and the alienation inherent to individuation, becoming a full-orbed, individual person.

My interest here is a less theoretical and a more operational psychological perspective on Genesis 3. Let me paint it on a canvas stretched upon the structuralist model of Piaget, Kohlberg, Erikson, Fowler, and Fuller.[4] If one takes the story of the fall seriously as an element in a paradigm for general human psychological development, it may be seen to describe a crucial stage in human growth from the childlikeness of Eden to mature building of God's kingdom and the fashioning of cultural responsibility. In that growth process, the story plays the role equivalent to the human process of adolescent disengagement from parents, an inherently healthy and necessary process.

That personal adolescent separation process for humans is normally fraught with a good deal of anxiety and pain. That same strain is evident in Adam and Eve in this story. They have significant anxiety about the presence of the forbidden tree. It represents the boundaries and limitations of a self and the primitive nature of childhood. Their anxiety is about making a decision, wise or forbidden, conforming or exploratory, obedient or learning. This speaks of the human challenge to lay hold of the unknown of the future as we grow and develop. The appearance of the tempting serpent induces anxiety. He represents the developing ego's awareness of the ambiguity of life and the need for individuation and self-actualization.

The double seduction of Eve and Adam is fraught with anxiety, as is the awareness of the orphaning nature of being cut loose from parental authority and care. Finally, the realization of human mortality is the spectre that lurks behind all our pain and pathology, according to this story. Will we surely die if we launch out into the unknown and invest ourselves in learning, investigation, and experimentation? Everything about the story heads toward intense anxiety about God's death threat. All these various forms of anxiety are internalized as shame and guilt, as children always do.

One of the most interesting elements of the fall story is what it tells us about Adam and Eve's anxiety *before* the fall, when the womblike paradise was still intact. The story seems to emphasize that recognition of this is important in understanding human nature. It tells us something about what it means to be made in the image of God: a mover, shaker, decider, creator like God is. Adam is described as finding himself alone in the garden and sufficiently needy and confused that he looked for a mate or companion among the animals. He found none adequate or appropriate. God noted the stress and anxiety and created Eve as a help appropriate to his neediness. Obviously that means that she filled some condition of anguished incompleteness in Adam and thereby reduced his stress and anxiety. We do not read that she had any inadequacies.

One can imagine that Adam had considerable stress from numerous directions in Eden. There was the pressure of responsibility to keep the garden, to find appropriate companionship, to manage his awakening sexuality, to name the animals, to fashion a meaningful relationship with his wife when he found her, to deal with her ultimate choice of liberation and independence in consorting with the serpent and eating of the forbidden fruit, to go along with her seductive proposal to do the same lest he lose her, and to obey and love God in a world where the manner of doing so was fairly ambiguous, and in any case, complex. The man was under pressure.

It must be noted that all this was going on before the fall, so his anxiety was not the consequence of sin or disobedience. His anxiety and suffering were clearly the consequence of his being a person with unexplored potential and possibilities. His stress preceded his disobedience or sin and had to do with his awakening awareness of himself as an individual person with choices. It is inherent to his nature and all human nature. It is inevitable to human existence, because humans grow and development brings change. Change means the future is unknown. The Hebrews saw that and related it to the human potential for bad decisions. So they told the old Mesopotamian story in a new way to describe the truth about our painful nature and experience. When we read that mythic narrative of 3,000 years ago we recognize it as our own story. But why is it a story about sex and seduction?

I think it is not the intent of the story to give sex a bad name. Sex is symbolic here of all our vulnerabilities and neediness. This is not a story about God having a negative view of sex. He designed it for all organisms on this planet and instructed humans to be fruitful and multiply (Genesis 1:28).

Becoming aware of and coming to terms with our sexuality is symbolic of all the challenges humans face in exploring the unknown in life. Sexual awakening comes in adolescence along with individuation and disengagement from parents and dependency. That is a time when we move from the dependence of childhood and childishness to individual development and independence. The fall story, with its seductive sexual undercurrent, represents the perpetual human quest for crossing boundaries into new worlds of exploration, knowledge, relationships, and experience. Since we do not know in advance how to do this, it is a journey with considerable risk and potential gratification.

As soon as God announced the presence and import of the forbidden tree, a state of dissonance existed in Adam. He perceived that his destiny was open-ended and required decision making by him and Eve. He recognized that he possessed the potential for change and for negative or positive growth. The anxiety increased in intensity as the story recounts Adam and Eve struggling with the essential decision about their unknown and challenging future. The pressure of that anxiety is further increased as they contemplate, quite correctly, the possibility of being like God, knowing both good and evil. That is our human predicament.

The decision Adam made to explore the new world of being like God, functioned psychologically as an anxiety-reduction mechanism. It freed his psyche for better function, coping, and growth. Was his decision constructive or destructive for him and the human race? Is the sexual exploration of adolescence constructive or destructive? Is the painful process of adolescent disengagement from parents constructive or destructive as an anxiety-reduction mechanism? Should we look at adolescent alienation, pain, and anxiety as difficult but inevitable stages in the evolution of persons or as an unfortunate aberration of a sinful or destructive behavior that makes God exceedingly disturbed?

Seward Hiltner (1972) contended persuasively that the Genesis 3 narrative is a metaphor of the human maturation process, producing individuation and responsible personhood as independent agents of constructive action. He therefore urged that the story is a report on the human psychological process of asserting human will against the will of God. He claimed that such an act was necessary for humanity and is necessary for individuals, because saying "Yes" to God in commitment has no meaning or content if it is impossible to say "No." Maturity requires the ego strength and volition to forge the power and right to disengage from authority and dependency, in order to give significance to the intent or behavior of recommitment to "the other" as an adult agent. Hiltner's notion reflects the paradigm of adolescent disengagement and assumes that it requires a willful negative act, testing one's own strength over against the pressures toward conformity represented by the expectations we think we perceive in our parents, society, and God. Without this disengagement there can be no growth. The sexual implications are simple and straightforward. Without sexual experimentation, individuation, and exploration we have no good knowledge of our own real sexual natures, needs, and styles.

Obviously life moves progressively toward differentiation and individuation. Healthy children move from fusion with the mother in the womb, to pubescent individuation, to adolescent disengagement, to re-fusion with parents as friendly adult peers. The dramatic contrasts and even dissonances of normal development are necessary in order to achieve a genuine individuality. The re-fusion as adult peers is a return toward union, commitment, and cherishing in which neither parent nor child feels constrained by the relationship; and both are thus free to choose it, and to do so out of their strengths, not their dependencies or obligations. The same is true of sex and love in a committed relationship.

It is not quite clear whether the Hebrews intended the fall story to describe a step taken in the best possible manner. There seems to be adequate reason to feel that they saw Adam's action as a failure, at least in style. Howard Clinebell's championing what he calls growth psychology emphasized that the negative aspects of human nature and the human pilgrimage are necessary elements or stages in an evolutionary continuum of growth.[5] It is not certain, I think, whether he would see the fall story as commenting significantly upon our real human predicament, since his model suggests a growth line that moves rather smoothly from conception to birth, childhood, adolescence, and maturity without the sort of psychological discontinuity that the fall story or a painful adolescent disengagement represents, with all its usual sexual overtones and undertones.

If the adolescent differentiation process is seen as paradigmatic of the fall story or vice versa, it is useful to ask whether Adam might have done it in any better way. Does humanity need to express so much disjunction and experience so much explosive revolution or alienation and loss in order to achieve personhood and growth? Was it a constructive or destructive anxiety-reduction mechanism? When looking at this text through the psychological lens it is tempting to say that Adam chose the best course, and in view of his limited knowledge and experience, the only one he really had available. That would be a way of saying that the loss and alienation we all experience from the termination of our secure world in the womb to the loss of childhood by adolescent individuation, and the consequent distortions in our psychosocial world, are virtually inevitable to our growth and development. This would then be true spiritually, socially, psychologically, intellectually, and sexually.

As we grow, our limited knowledge, experience, and wisdom prevent us from choosing other than the painful and alienating experimental courses. Such an interpretation of this story and of the story of life seems to make sense. This hypothesis implies that pain was inevitable in God's world from the beginning and inherent to the created order of things. It implies further that the choice could not have been different if growth and maturation were to evolve out of the primitive and childlike naivete of the Eden-womb; whether one is speaking of the individual human's development or the maturation of humanity as a community.

It is clear, however, that the Israelite editor of this myth, as well as his or her Mesopotamian antecedents who formulated the earlier version, intended to explain the problem of evil and human disorder by asserting that humanity had made a bad choice. That does not imply that some decisive act by Adam to move him from naivete to maturity was not necessary. Neither does it mean that nothing constructive toward real growth came out of Adam's and Eve's actual decision. It only contends that his decision was a transitional act unnecessarily fraught with self-defeat, rebellion, and alienation. The Hebrews saw it as a destructive anxiety-reduction mechanism, insofar as they sensed it in those terms. Unfortunately, this confusion and ambiguity has plagued the human quest for sexual and spiritual identity ever since the influence of this story assumed so large a role in our worldview.

That does not erase the fact that the fall, that is, maturing individuation, has constructive, freedom-affording results for humans. It moved humanity, even in the mythic story as the Hebrews cast it, from the naiveté of domesticated persons to the sophistication of responsible agents taking charge of their world. Similarly, adolescence may be handled unnecessarily rebelliously by some teenagers but lead out to a growth process that results in profoundly healthy relationships with parents, authorities, and traditions later on. Sexual exploration may be injudicious and fraught with ignorant clumsiness, but the very experience gained by it may prove highly valuable in constructing more profoundly wholesome relationships as one matures in relationship building.

The fall story represents one symbolic option for implementing the necessary and inevitable differentiation process. The Hebrews thought of it as a destructive option. The implication is that Adam, as a character in this dramatic myth, might have exercised an equally growth-inducing, rather than destructive, act of will and ego strength by choosing to affirm God's will and value system, *for Adam's own well-motivated and independent reasons.* The implication is that we might well do the same in our sexual exploration, to our own comfort and advantage. Presumably that would have been as initiatory, independent, and individuating an act toward growth as disobedience proved to be. It would also, presumably, have led to less self-defeating, *though adequately self-affirming* consequences. Moreover, the meaning of this for human history is the implication that the distortion, pain, alienation, and sickness with which humans have responded to generic anxiety through history were not inevitable elements of the growth process of the human race. The implication would be that humans have made many bad decisions of style and action. The story is suggesting that such decisions can be made more wisely, redemptively, and faithfully, with healthier consequences. Some adolescents and adults seem able to do just that.

It is, of course, intriguing to speculate, in terms of the story's literary structure and psychological freight, just how the narrative could have unfolded to its denoument, had the author or editor chosen such a benign outcome. How would the story of mankind then proceed in the narrative? Could it adequately account for the problem of pain? Would it be at all interesting and dramatic, as it is in its present form? Could the author actually "get out of his story," that is, bring it to a workable end? How would he have gotten his characters offstage? It is really difficult to imagine what alternative story lines would have worked in terms of the literary and psychological requirements of the passage. What if the real state of affairs in the human psyche, spirit, and world of external experience were such as to prompt or permit a different mythic story in Genesis 3? What if the story could have represented humanity as reaching forward, within the will of God, for individuality, maturity, and wisdom; for knowledge of being like God in comprehending the world inside out, in knowing God as he now knows us? Cooperative growth with God and exploration of the possibilities of human destiny in tranquility is not a story that rings true to the human experience of dissonance, alienation, and disease, but suggests a redemptive alternative that might have been from the beginning, if we were not so badly distorted by generic anxiety.

Of course, a major problem with such a proposal lies in the fact that none of us knows how to do life in advance. An interesting Afrikaans proverb says, "In the symphony of life no one gets the program music in advance." One of the most difficult aspects of human life is the fact that you have to do it right in the middle of it. What if the ancient Israelites had inserted into our Sacred Scriptures a foundational myth in which they had told the objective truth rather than the symbolic stories of Genesis 3 or 6? What if they had realized and narrated the story of humankind as that of an evolution from more primitive beginnings, rather than some perfect Eden? What if they had taught us from the outset to think of our roots, origins, and development as the human community as coming from a untrained and unequipped group of *Homo sapiens* who struggled to make the simplest sense out of a hard evolutionary process and ultimately achieved the wonderful sophistication to which humanity has come, despite the remaining flaws?

What if humans had always thought of themselves as surprisingly achieving creatures rather than "fallen" ones, working against the worst of odds, and building a world of relative humaneness, love, wisdom, learning, creativity, beauty and kindness? What if our loving and lovemaking, our sex and sensuality, had been cast from the beginning as the positive and beautiful thing that it is? That would have been the truth, and would have provided our sexual experimentation, exploration, achievement, and union a positive and celebrative aura, marking lovemaking as the supreme expression of the unique nature of human spirituality. This would have delivered our sexuality from its inherent anxiety and ambiguity and replaced our ambivalence and guilt about sex, intimacy, and vulnerability with healthy confidence and joyfulness.

Is our operating perspective, during the last 5,000 years as a human community, merely the consequence of the dominance in human culture of the negative and destructive cast of the Genesis 3 narrative, and the shadow it has laid upon all our thinking? Is it not possible, even likely, that that story has so shaped our thinking about ourselves that we have been unable to recognize that the human race has always really striven for constructive ego development within the will of God; limited only by our inadequacy of knowledge, wisdom, and opportunity; distorted only by our generic anxiety and loneliness? Is it not obvious that our problem is not that we are sinful or evil, but underdeveloped, under-evolved. It seems apparent that the discovery of the notion of unconditional grace is a move to definitively outflank Genesis 3 and move humanity into a story that has as its main theme the growth mode of self-actualization and human health within the economy of God.

As the story stands it declares that the individuating and sexually developing human should achieve health and growth by choosing, as an independent act of will and ego, to affirm and follow the "healthful" values of authorities, tradition, community norms, parental expectations, and other sources of encouragement toward conformity. Indeed, the narrative urges that that course, when expressing rather than compromising the individual's own authenticity, may be far less self-defeating, inefficient, erosive of health, and less painful than disengagement that strains relationships or maximizes confrontation, alienation, and grief-loss; aggravating generic human anxiety and loneliness and thus sickening us. Unfortunately the Genesis narrative gives us no hint of how that might have been done or what its results would look like in human history or human psycho-spirituality.

Perhaps Clinebell is really on the right track in deemphasizing the cataclysmic and alienating dimensions of human fallenness while placing all the emphasis upon the freedom for growth that humans as independent agents need and possess. His model implies that the fall speaks of a revolution and that, however descriptive that may be of actual perceived human experience, humans have the alternative option of an evolutionary growth response to anxiety. Donald Capps suggests that such life transitions as the fall story represents cause healthy persons to constantly reframe their perceptions of the meaning of exploratory experiences and anxiety so as to incorporate them into lives of constructive growth, sexually and spiritually.[6] It is our present task to transcend and outflank the negative outlook of those ancient stories of Genesis 3 and 6, and find again the beauty of sex and true humanity, without ambiguity, guilt, or anxiety.

Chapter 8

OLD TESTAMENT SEX LAWS: WOMEN AS PROPERTY VERSUS WOMEN AS AGENTS OF THEIR DESTINY

The Old Testament is, for the most part, an interesting read. Appreciated as great ancient literature or as a religious story, it is of genuine interest to a bright inquirer. The variety of literature and religious narrative is immense and surprisingly creative. We have in this ancient Hebrew collection a mixture of grand poetry, intriguing historical accounts, profound theological treatises, surprisingly cynical and tough-minded philosophical ruminations, and wild-eyed visionary expostulations.

That part of the OT that was most valued by the ancient people who crafted it and savored its aesthetic beauty and spiritual inspiration was the Torah, namely the first five books of the OT or *Hebrew Bible*. The ancient Israelites knew them as the Five Books of Moses, and so they came to be called the Pentateuch. Those five books contained the main stories about a covenant of grace and goodness between God and the Israelites, in which he guaranteed that he would be their gracious God, no matter what happened, and they would be his people, no matter what they did (Genesis 12 and 17). It was in the Torah, also, that the summary of God's expectations of the Israelites was recorded in the Decalogue, the Ten Commandments.

Most every Israelite had a fairly clear sense, throughout the centuries, of what the Decalogue required. However, just as was the case with Adam and Eve and the forbidden tree in the Garden of Eden, so also God's imposition of expectations, commandments, and restraints upon the Israelites caused them anxiety. The Decalogue set boundaries upon them and some of the Israelites were neurotic enough to fear that they might accidentally break one of those commandments and wreak havoc upon themselves and their world. The boundaries set for them made them fear that God was a threat, caused them to exaggerate the implied penalty for disobedience, and so prompted them to view the Decalogue with fear and trembling.

Consequently, the ancient priests of Israel devised a large number of regulations to put a hedge around the Decalogue and to mark off Israel, as a people, as different from their Canaanite counterparts of other religious affiliation. They included in the Torah 613 more commandments, *mitzvoth,* in addition to the Decalogue. These offered prescriptions for moral behavior as well as ceremonial and civic regulations. Among those additional commandments there were many that had to do with sexual behavior, particularly sexual behavior by women and toward women. The *mitzvoth* spelled out what behavior was appropriate to the special people of God and what behavior was *toevah,* an abomination because it was behavior practiced by the Canaanites. These 613 *mitzvoth* were called the Holiness Code in the Torah.

Many of the sex laws in the Holiness Code can be found in Leviticus (Leviticus Sex Texts or LST) but there are also a number of them in the book of Deuteronomy (Deuteronomy Sex Texts or DST). In fact, the list is as follows: Leviticus 15:18, 24, 33b; 18: 1–30; 19:20–22, 29; 20:10–21; 21:9 and Deuteronomy 5:18; 21:10–14; 22:13—23:1; 23:17–18; 24:1–4; 25:5–10; 27:20–23; 28:30. These laws are of great interest from a number of points of view. For our purposes it is mainly the pattern of similarity and difference between the sex laws in Deuteronomy and those in Leviticus that tell us a great deal about the Bible's most ancient sexual codes.

For a long time Bible students thought all the laws in both Bible books (DST and LST) were part of the same code, but recently scholars have demonstrated that they are two different, though related, sex codes. The sex laws in Deuteronomy are generally considered to be older than those in Leviticus. That makes the contrast between them especially worth studying to see how the ideas of lawful treatment of women developed in ancient Israel from one period to the next.[1] "Marked differences distinguish the treatment of women in LST from the treatment of women in DST . . . whereas the concern of LST is classificatory, the concern of DST is proprietary. These differences in concerns construct corresponding differences in the conceptualization of women in the two groups of texts" (D. L. Ellens, p. iv).

While the two codes generally address the same kinds of sexual behavior, they differ in the outlook they take toward those acts, the manner in which they speak of the sex act, and the way in which the law applies to the specific person and act involved. The codes are concerned about women being marginalized in society, women being turned into objects rather than being treated as persons, and the way in which women are regulated and/or protected by the law code in LST and in DST.

In the older code in DST, women are generally viewed as an important part of the Israelite community, but as a property of their fathers and then of their husbands. This property-character of a woman is spelled out specifically in terms of her sexual qualities. These are designated as the property of her male householder, and by extension, the property of the community. In the DST women are rarely referred to as persons or agents in their own right, with control over and responsibility for their own behavior. When they are referred to as agents in the DST, their agency has to do with their responsibility to protect the purity and sanctity of their own sexuality as property of their male householders. The exercise of this agency by a women is specifically to ensure the tranquility and security of the Israelite home and family; thereby insuring the tranquility and shalom, that is, the peace and prosperity, of the entire community or nation.

Things are different in the newer LST which was created sometime between the Babylonian Exile and shortly before the time of Philo Judaeus, Jesus, and Josephus (500–50 B.C.E.). In this "new" code women are usually viewed as agents of their own destiny, who are directly responsible, through proper sexual behavior, for the tranquility and shalom of the Israelite community or nation; rather than being indirectly responsible for the peace and prosperity of Israel by behaving in a way that protected the property of their householder (father or husband) and their family. Thus their responsibility for their own behavior, sexually and otherwise, is in some degree similar in kind to that of male agents in society; though it is never similar in degree, since in both the earlier and later codes women are, nonetheless, marginalized, turned into objects, and shifted to a different stance than men in their relationship to the laws which regulate them. Women never completely escape the role of property and always remain in the mode of shaping their own behavior, not for their own freedom but for the benefit of the society. So in these two sex codes women never move out of subservience to their male householders and to society, even though in LST they are assigned agency and control over their own behavior. When we contemplate the advances in Israelite sexual codes and ethics from the DST in about 1250 B.C.E. to the LST in, say, 250 B.C.E., we certainly find it remarkable that the progress was as enlightened as it was, primitive though it still remained.

In her address to these issues, D. L. Ellens sets the stage for her analysis by declaring helpfully that

> The writers of the biblical laws, like the writers of other legal corpora throughout history, considered the regulation of sex to be of some importance. Throughout history such regulation has been part of the total jurisprudential effort to preserve peace and order in any society. James A. Brundage states that "every human society attempts to control sexual behavior, since sex represents a rich source of conflicts that can disrupt orderly social processes." Tikva Frymer-Kensky's observations with respect to sex in the Bible coincide with Brundage's remarks. She asserts that sexuality in the Bible has to do with "social control and behavior." Its concern is "who with whom and when." (p. 1)[2]

These ancient biblical sex codes spell out the powers, duties, and rights of individual women. The difference between a woman being treated as a real person and being treated as a property has to do with the degree to which she possesses those powers, duties, and rights. If she has little of that, she is an object and mere property. If she has a lot of those prerogatives, she is more of a person in her own right. "The ratio of an individual's entitlements to his or her obligations defines the level of personhood."[3] The sex codes in Deuteronomy and Leviticus set the legal boundaries that spell these things out. Trespass of the laws that made women property of males (DST) was a sin of greed or selfishness. In the Leviticus texts, however, the issue at stake is a woman maintaining the purity of her sexuality for the sake of the shalom of the community. Any sin regarding that was the offense of impurity and uncleanness. Breach of the legal boundaries set by these two codes is not always distinctly either a property or purity offense. It may sometimes be both. D. L. Ellens points out carefully that in the two sex codes in the *Hebrew Bible,* "purity is always in some way a component of the infractions of the property sex laws, property is sometimes absent as a component of the infractions of the purity sex laws" (p. 31).

The first biblical text in the code in Deuteronomy is chapter 5, verses 18 and 21a. These concern the commandment against adultery and coveting one's neighbor's wife. This issue is treated in chapter 9 so we move forward here to Deuteronomy 21: 10–14.

> When you go forth to war . . . and see among the captives a beautiful woman, and you have desire for her and would take her for yourself as wife, then you shall bring her home to your house, and she shall shave her head and pare her nails. And she shall put off her captive's garb, and shall remain

in your house and bewail her father and her mother a full month; after that you may go in to her, and be her husband, and she shall be your wife. Then, if you have no delight in her, you shall let her go where she will; but you shall not sell her for money, you shall not treat her as a slave, since you have humiliated her.

It requires no persuasive argument to see that in this teaching of the Bible, a woman taken as a captive is treated as property. There are, however, a number of interesting things that must be said about this woman and this situation. The woman involved is not a member of the Israelite community, but an alien imported into an Israelite household. It is clear that there is some specific interest in this law to protect the woman from wanton abuse, rape, or exploitation. The man who has taken her as property is required to bring her into his home and make her a legitimate part of his household, allow her to grieve for a standard Near Eastern period, refrain from sexual intercourse with her for one month, and not treat her as a form of property that can be for sale. She remains his property and a member of his house, or she is to be a free woman.

Undoubtedly, there were a number of reasons for this regulation. It prevented impetuous behavior on the part of the male, which might physically damage the woman. It attempted to limit the emotional and spiritual damage she sustained. It gave her a month to demonstrate that she was not pregnant by a former liaison among the enemies of Israel, thereby guaranteeing that any progeny produced by her would be a true child of Israel. Her humiliation must be compensated for, in the case that she is set free, by her being treated as a person with agency and control over her own destiny. Of course, one must ask what the fate of such a woman would be, after she had been captured, used, and discarded by an Israelite male. Widows or unsponsored single women had a difficult time in the ancient Near East. All in all, this code may have been more humane than that of most Near Eastern codes of the time, but it seems rather unenlightened for all that, in this day and age.

D. L. Ellens notes that the main concern here is the smooth process of acquiring a wife as property under "difficult circumstances, in which the end is achieved by the act of sexual intercourse. This act made the Israelite male the owner of exclusive right to the woman's sexuality, both against the claims of any other man and against her own claims for independent control of her own sexuality. Thus, Deut. 21:10–14 supports the thesis that, in Deuteronomy, where sexuality and women intersect, the primary focus and concern is the woman's sexuality as the property of the man" (p. 275).

A similar picture is painted by the very next chapters of the Bible, Deuteronomy 22:13–30. The context of this passage is a set of laws that require a man to look after the well-being of his brother's person and property if he sees it endangered. This text, itself, concerns a number of different cases. The first is a situation in which a man has taken a wife and then does not want her anymore so he makes the claim that she was not a virgin and so ruins her reputation. In such a case, her family is to bring the evidence that proves she was a virgin and the man is to be fined heavily and is required to keep her as his wife and not divorce her. However, if the charge against her is correct, she is to be stoned to death.

The text continues with the case of a man having sexual intercourse with another man's wife. In this case it is not referred to as adultery, as it is in Deuteronomy 7:18 and 21a, but it is described as a corrupting evil. The sentence is that both persons must be put to death. The third case is one in which a virgin who is engaged to be married is taken, in the streets of a town, to have sex with a man to whom she is not engaged. Both are to be stoned to death: she for not crying for help, and he because he violated his neighbor's wife. If, however, as in the fourth case in this passage, this same scene takes place in the open country, where crying for help can solicit no assistance, the man shall be put to death but the virgin exonerated. In every one of these cases the sentence is designed to "purge evil from the society." That is, the punishment or threat of the law is to ensure good order to the society and sexual purity to the community and its families.

Two more cases are cited. If a man meets a virgin who is not engaged to anyone and he has sex with her and they are caught at it, he must pay her father a heavy fine and keep the woman forever as his wife. Finally, no man may take his father's wife or be in anyway sexually intimate with her. Male property and female sexual purity are both at stake in these cases and protected by these laws. Women are both property and agents responsible for their own sexual purity. That has significance for the stability and good order of the family and society, keeping evil at bay.

This concern is given a religious cast in Deuteronomy 23:17–18 where we read, "There shall be no cult prostitute of the daughters of Israel, neither shall there be a cult prostitute of the sons of Israel. You shall not bring the hire of a harlot . . . into the house of the Lord your God in payment of a vow; for . . . these are an abomination to the Lord your God." This does not speak directly of woman as property, but implies it in the commandment that if one owns a whore and gains profit from that it is an evil in God's sight. Cult prostitution and financing the temple treasury by it was a Canaanite religious practice. It was forbidden in Israel because it eroded the distinctive character of the people of Yahweh, as we shall also see in chapter 11 regarding homosexual behavior by heterosexuals in religious worship practices.

Deuteronomy 24:1–4 deals with divorce and remarriage to the divorced woman. It speaks of a man who married and found the woman had some indecency in her so he divorced her. She married another and he found likewise and divorced her. Then he died. In this case her first husband is not to take her to wife again. That would "bring guilt upon the land which the Lord your God gives you for an inheritance." The Bible does not specify why this would be an evil thing about which to be guilty, but it implies that this complex case would confuse the property rights and probably it intends to say that this would also be an impure thing to do. *Guilt* is an interesting and a bit of a perplexing word for the Bible to use here. D. L. Ellens claims that "The law in Deut. 24:1–4 concerns property issues related to special circumstances of divorce. The law is not about sexual impurity and does not regulate sexual intercourse" (p. 386).

Deuteronomy 25:5–10 is a law designed to establish forever the name of a dead man. This is the passage Jesus' critics, the rather playful Sadducees, put before him, asking whose wife a woman would be who had married seven brothers in succession and had all of them die on her. The law requires that if a married man dies without a male heir, his brother shall get that dead man's wife pregnant and name the first-born son for his dead brother, whose heir and name-carrier that son shall be. The law further specifies that if the brother refuses, the woman is to take her case to the elders and they are to negotiate with the man who has this responsibility for his dead brother. If he still refuses, the woman is to jerk off his shoe and spit in his face. He is then to be called throughout Israel, in perpetuity, "The guy who got jerked off."

This law is about the property and inheritance of the dead man. The woman is an object to be used in this process. Protecting the dead man's entitlement warrants turning the woman into such an object, according to this law. Her sexuality as the property of her dead husband is protected as the property of his estate. In so far as she acts as a self-determining agent in this passage, she is doing so as a component of that estate and its proper adjudication, not as the executor of that estate. She, and particularly her sexuality and fertility, are part of the property. This law is about property and contracts. The same is true of the series of cursing commandments in Deuteronomy 27:19–26. In verses 20, 22, and 23, the cursing laws are about sex. "Cursed is he who lies with his father's wife for he has uncovered her who belongs to his father . . . Cursed is he who lies with his sister, whether the daughter of his father or the daughter of his mother. . . . Cursed is he who lies with his mother-in-law. . . ." The other curses in this passage are exactly the same but are about other kinds of property, animals, other persons, neighbors, widows and orphans, sojourners, and the like. These laws are not designed to protect a woman or her sexuality in itself. They are designed to protect the property rights of the person to whom the woman belongs (see D. L. Ellens, p. 432).

The final text in the DST is simple. Deuteronomy 28:30 declares that if Israel does not keep these laws of protecting female sexuality as property, "You shall betroth a wife, and another man shall lie with her; you shall build a house, and you shall not dwell in it; you shall plant a vineyard, and you shall not use the fruit of it." The sex code of Deuteronomy is designed to keep the property claims clear to ensure peace and prosperity for the society. Women are property of a fairly precious and significant type. The violation of this property can wreak surprising havoc on the entire society. D. L. Ellens summarizes this as follows. "Thus, woman, marginalized and objectified, is . . . sexual property of the man. . . . The curse places upon the lawbreaker the catastrophe of the 'loss' of this property. The primary concern is, thus, to guard the law of Yahweh by threatening such disasters as the loss by one man of his sexual property, in the form of the woman who belongs to him, at the hands of *another* man" (443).

As we turn to the Levitical code, as I suggested above, we discern the anticipated shift in focus spelled out above. The first text in that code is five verses from Leviticus 15 (18–19, 24, 32–33).

> If a man lies with a woman and has an emission of semen, both of them shall bathe themselves in water, and be unclean until the evening. When a woman has a discharge of blood which is her regular discharge from her body, she shall be in her impurity for seven days and whoever touches her shall be unclean until the evening. . . . And if any man lies with her, and her impurity is on him, he shall be unclean seven days; and every bed on which he lies shall be unclean. . . . This is the law for him who has a discharge and for him who has an emission of semen, becoming unclean thereby; also for . . . the man who lies with a woman who is unclean.

Property issues, related to women or unrelated to them, are not the concern in Leviticus 15. The issues here are purity and uncleanness, particularly as related to bodily emissions of men and women. Genital behavior is of concern here only in terms of purity, and that equally with respect to men and women. Women are, nonetheless, marginalized and turned into objects by the way in which the texts view everything from the male point of view. Men are the primary actors in the scenarios and women are the objects "out there" at whom the text is looking, since the view is from the male perspective and posture.

> All this suggests an interesting conceptual movement with respect to woman in the text of Lev. 15. The language-depicting-the-sex-act portrays woman as object and man as subject. The structure of the chapter, however, portrays them as equal with respect to purity issues. The evidence with respect to purity issues connected to intercourse demonstrates that women like men are subjects responsible for maintaining their own purity and the purity of the community. Furthermore, this concern for purity is not weighted as a greater concern for the welfare of the man than the welfare of the woman. Woman's action and state of being are as important as those of the man. The community's welfare depends equally upon the initiative, discernment and trustworthy action of men and women, with respect to their discharges. . . . Clearly, we have before us in the text an interesting conceptual movement which understands woman to be circumscribed by man in a variety of ways and also sees her to be equal with respect to a particular issue. . . . Purity of the community is uppermost in the mind of the writer. The author's inten-tion is not to forbid the flows or the acts described. Rather, his intention is to mediate impurity when it occurs . . . in men as well as women . . . with remarkable gender equity. (D. L. Ellens, pp. 91–92)

So property issues are not at stake in Leviticus 15. The Israelites have come a long way by the time of these sexual laws within the Holiness Code of the Torah. Unfortunately, nonetheless, women are still marginal-ized objects. Though they have some power as agents over their own des-tiny and they have some responsibility for their own selves and sexuality, they are continually viewed and valued from the perspective of the way they are related to males. They do not have value in their own right.

This is even more evident in Leviticus 18:6–20. The entire section of the Bible is summarized in the first verse cited, "None of you shall approach any one near of kin to him to uncover nakedness. I am the Lord." The list of those to whom this law applies is long and detailed, including every one up and down the ladder of generations and as wide as first cousins. The references all protect a woman's sexuality on the grounds that she is some other man's property, for example, "You shall not uncover the nakedness of your father's wife. It is your father's nakedness" (v. 8).

Wegner claimed that while some of the women listed in Leviticus 18 are not blood relatives, they are all sexual property of a relative, so the incest taboos protect private property as much as sexual propriety.[4] How-ever Douglas contends that the burden of this passage is the claim that incest and adultery are against holiness because they violate right order. Holiness is more a matter of specifying what boundaries separate various behaviors than a matter of protecting the rights of males.[5] D. L. Ellens thinks that the text itself is responsible for this surprising difference of interpretation (p. 93). She suggests that while Douglas seems closer to the truth in this case, by asserting that the laws in this passage are designed for boundary setting so as to preserve holiness and right order; nonetheless, women are marginalized and treated like objects, in the sense that the author addresses a male audience exclusively, and talks about women as though they are something "out there." Women are passive receivers, moved around like checkers. "The male ego of the text mediates whatever instruction the author intends for the female Israelite. Her responsibilities under the law, with one exception, are only implied and all but entirely fade from the explicit text. The resulting, initial impression for the reader is that the law guards the sexual property of the man who is himself the sole guardian of sexual propriety" (pp. 93–94). She calls this the gender-asymmetry of this text. It is lopsided in its orientation upon male interests rather than male and female interests.

Nonetheless, D. L. Ellens claims, there are indications in the way in which the text speaks of the sexual behavior that subtly imply agency and responsibility on the part of the woman in her own right. "While her status is highly circumscribed by and dependent on the man, she too is responsible to the law" (p. 136). She draws this out further by contending that the set of cases about incest and adultery in this passage illustrate the woman's dependence upon and subordination to men, but not her lack of responsibility. While the woman is marginalized and treated like an object, she is, by implication, described in her relationship to the law as having control and responsibility as an agent of the maintenance of her own purity, and not seen primarily as property (p. 137). As regards a woman's agency in this passage, Ellens's argument here is very subtle and rather thinly supported by the actual Bible text, it seems to me. However, the fact that it is the purity of the woman and her sexuality, and not property, that is at stake here, seems more obvious.

Leviticus 19:20–22 is quite different from the set of regulations in chapter 18. It concerns sex with slaves.

> If a man lies carnally with a woman who is a slave, betrothed to another man and not yet ransomed or given her freedom, an inquiry shall be held. They shall not be put to death, because she was not free; but he shall bring a guilt offering for himself to the Lord . . . and the priest shall make atonement for him . . . and the sin which he has committed shall be forgiven him.

This passage is different than all the others in the Leviticus sex code because in this one the woman involved and her sexuality are both individual items of property. A man owns this woman as a slave and he owns her sexuality because she is his slave. In this case the owner of both has assigned ownership of her sexuality to another man by giving her in marriage to him.

The culprit in this case is a third man who has violated the property rights of both of the other men in that he has involved himself sexually with the woman who belongs to them, thus violating both one man's slave without his permission, and another man's sexual possession, without a right to do so. His punishment is not death, because this is not a capital crime. That implies that the violation of the law of God is not the violation of the woman's sexuality as a person who has a right to control her sexuality. It is a violation of the law of God against violating another man's property. Therefore the matter is resolved by his paying a fine and all is forgiven. D. L. Ellens argues that the issue at stake here is not that this is a regulation about either the abuse of a woman or the violation of property but about how the violator's status within the law of holiness shall be restored. He is to pay a fine and that's that!

> Two kinds of boundaries . . . are relevant to the case. The first boundary guards the woman as the property of the master. The second boundary is similar to the boundaries of betrothal and marriage which guard a woman's sexuality for use by a single man. Although the woman is indisputably the legal property of one man—the master; and although her sexuality is "assigned" to another man, the primary concern of the law is not the rights of either man to her or to her sexuality. Rather, the primary concern of the law is restoration of the male perpetrator to a state of purity. (p. 130)

Because the woman in this case is not an Israelite, but a slave imported from elsewhere, she is not presented as an agent having any degree of power or control over her destiny, socially or sexually. That is not the issue before us here. She is not an agent in this scripture, but no one would expect her to be. She is a slave. Everything about her person is owned by her master. In this sense, of course, she is marginalized as a person and as a figure present in but of no value as a person to the Israelite society. She is, thus, turned into an object of property. Indeed, she is turned so much into an object that her being a piece of property never becomes the issue at stake here. It is simply assumed as a normal state of affairs. She is used as slaves are. No question on that issue. But the question is, how can the man who used her get right with the law, since he did something against another man, that is, unlawfully invaded his property. He can get right with the law by paying a fine. The woman, as woman, is an accident to the story, and of no count. It would have been the same had she been the man's dog, or plow, or haystack that was violated. So the story is about purity of the man who does wrong, not about the property or purity of the men or woman wronged.

The twenty-ninth verse of Leviticus 19 is a case of pimping your daughter as a prostitute. "Do not profane your daughter by making her a harlot, lest the land fall into harlotry and the land become full of wickedness." This case is also about purity. That is plain from the fact that this daughter is unbetrothed and unmarried. So her sexuality belongs to her father. But this law does not protect her sexuality as property of her father. It protects her sexuality by limiting her father's control over it to the requirements of maintaining purity. "The primary concern is thus preservation of the purity of the woman rather than protection of her sexuality as property" (D. L. Ellens, p. 160). This is typical of the LST in contrast to the DST.

The law speaks only to the father and does not address the daughter as a person involved in this matter. Thus she is marginalized to the periphery of the conversation or the scene, so to speak. She is also spoken of as an object out there which can be moved around in various postures by someone else, that is, the male agent, her father. But her father may not just move her around or use her as he pleases. This law does not protect his property rights regarding her (D. L. Ellens, p. 171). The father is constrained by whatever is necessary to maintain her purity. That is the issue here: her purity and hence the purity of the land.

Leviticus 20:10–21 picks up the theme consistently present in the LST, that is, the maintenance of the purity of the community and, by extension, the land. The impurity with which this scripture is preoccupied is that of adultery with a relative, kin of a near relative, or a neighbor. The examples that are given are numerous and varied, including sex with a neighbor's wife, with a relative as close or closer than first cousins, with a woman and her daughter, with a woman in her menstrual time, and the like. This section of the Bible ends with the declaration regarding such behavior, that "it is impurity." This passage seems a repeat of Leviticus 18, and contains a more overt statement that the main issue here is the protection of the purity of women and the good order of the society, not her role as property of some male. However, in all of these Levitical regulations it is disturbing to a modern-day Bible reader that it is never the woman in the story who is addressed. She is always talked about as an object in a conversation between the Lord and the males of the society. This indicates the marginalization of women to the periphery of crucial matters of the society; and demonstrates that a woman is managed by the males who "possess" her, though she too, by implication is a responsible agent accountable to the law of purity.

This theme of purity is even more pronounced in the injunction regarding the daughter of a priest, who if she "plays the harlot" profanes herself and her father, the priest. The penalty announced by Leviticus 21 is that she shall be burned to death, thus purifying her father, the priesthood, and the land. This injunction is not addressed to the woman but to the male priests, marginalizing her as one to talk about, worry about, and manage. Nonetheless, "the fact that her actions constitute the infraction suggests that she is also implicitly addressed. As in all the prostitution laws, the sex act . . . is not explicitly depicted. Furthermore, in this law, the woman is also not objectified" (D. L. Ellens, p. 220).

This text makes it clear that should the daughter of a priest become a whore, it is something which she herself chooses and a course of behavior she causes herself to follow. This implies that she is the agent in charge of her course of action and she is responsible to the law for her actions. While the purity of both herself and her father is at stake, in terms of keeping the regulations of good order in the society, that conformity which purity demands depends completely upon her and cannot be accomplished by anyone except herself. So she is the sole agent of this infraction and of its prevention. Action against her as the sole agent is the only legitimate punishment, namely, that she be executed for her profaning the community, the land, her father and his priesthood, and herself. Whereas she is her father's property by reason of other laws in the holiness code, this law has nothing to do with or raises no issue in the question of property. It is exclusively a matter of purity and her responsible agency in it. The issue is her purity for the sake of her father's sanctity, and by implication, that of the priesthood.

The OT sex laws are of great significance to us because of the way in which they created a conscious and unconscious view of women that has been associated with the authority of our Sacred Scriptures for 3,000 years. This view holds women as objects and marginalizes them in large part from the central roles in society in determining their own destiny. Until recently this view promoted the official understanding that women were a kind of property of their husbands, for them to manage, care for, and utilize. The official notion regarding this seems to be eroding somewhat, but at the operational level it is not clear that much has changed. The feminist movement has championed women's freedom, independence, agency, and empowerment; but it has not solved the problem. It has alienated men and women from each other, leaving a large percentage of both unable to establish significant relationships, build marriages, bear children, and live communal lives.

This perspective was imported into the Christian community and entrenched in the church's mindset and practice from the rise of male domination of the leadership of the Christian movement and of the priesthood of the orthodox church. In the early church (33–250 C.E.), there was a large percentage of female leadership. This is evident from the report of Paul's missionary journeys and the rise of the Gentile church in Asia Minor, Greece, and Rome. From the time of Constantine's creation of an orthodox unity of the church at Nicea in 325 C.E., and perhaps 50 to 100 years before that, male domination of the church increased and was firmly established.

This patriarchal outlook of the Imperial Church, from the time of Constantine's imperial empowerment of the church as the handmaiden of the Roman Empire, to the present day, has set the tone of how women are valued and treated. This is evident in recent decisions of the Roman Catholic Church that turn back the provisions of Vatican II and obstruct the advancement of women to their rightful place in the ministry of the church. Moreover, the inequity of the role, place, and rewards of women in the workforce and social order of the Western world today still give evidence of the way in which these ancient sex codes, among other corollary influences, have controlled our thought, belief, and practice, to the considerable disadvantage of women.

Moreover, the Christian community of the last 2,000 years is not the only aspect of human society blighted by the memory of these ancient codes entrenched in Sacred Scripture, in culture, and in the human unconscious. Three religions and their Sacred Scriptures derive from the *Hebrew Bible:* Rabbinic Judaism with its Torah, Christianity with its *Holy Bible,* and Islam with its *Qur'an.* All have been shaped by the devaluing attitude regarding women that is championed by the Holiness Code of the ancient Israelites. This disposition is particularly evident in Islam, with its repression of women as agents of their own destiny, its marginalization of women's participation in society in general by restricting their opportunity for education, their freedom of movement as persons in their world in which they must go about veiled and anonymous, and their management by males as though they were property. Only if we look this monster squarely in the eye will we get the kind of constructive change in the order of things in religious institutions, in Western society, and in the world that absolutely must come about. It is interesting that the societies least influenced by ancient Israelite religion, namely the Communist and post-Communist cultures, have been much more enlightened regarding the function of women as agents of their own persons and destinies than have Judaism, Christianity, and Islam.

Chapter 9

ADULTERY:
SEX AND MARRIAGE

Considering the fact that adultery is summarily denounced and forbidden in the ancient Israelite sex codes, it is of great interest how much adultery there is going on in the Bible among the Israelites. There is, of course, the very early story of Judah's adultery with Tamar in Genesis 38:15–16, and the even older story of Lot's sexual relations with his two daughters, committing a double adultery and a double incest in one fell swoop, so to speak (Genesis 19:30–36). Exodus 20 and Deuteronomy 5 are the two recordings of the Ten Commandments in the Bible and both Exodus 20:14 and Deuteronomy 5:18 declare, "You shall not commit adultery." Matthew 5:27 and 19:18 repeat and endorse this commandment. That is plain and simple; neither complicated nor negotiable. The Bible says that this commandment came by Moses from God at Mt. Sinai. While that is probably not to be taken literally, the Decalogue seems to have been in the Israelite tradition from the time of Moses. That would make its origin about 1250 B.C.E., at the latest.

What a lot of stories in the Bible from that point on that depict Israelites busy committing adultery! Jeremiah 3:8 and 23:14 claim that the whole society of Israel was committing adultery. Jesus said that we all commit adultery in that, "Whoever looks upon a woman to lust after her has committed adultery with her already in his heart" (Matthew 5:28). Presumably it works the other way around as well: a woman looking upon a man to lust. David committed adultery with Bathsheba and had her husband murdered (2 Samuel 11–12). David's son, Amnon, raped his half-sister Tamar, and whereas it is hard to tell from the text if this was also adultery, his abuse of her afterward was psychologically equivalent to David murdering Uriah (2 Samuel 13:1–19). In John 8:4 we have a story of a woman whom the authorities brought to Jesus because they had caught her in the act of adultery. Hosea had a wife who was constantly committing adultery (Hosea 1–3).

Of course, David repented of his sins of adultery and murder in anguish and sorrow (2 Samuel 12:13). This tragedy brought him to his knees, literally and metaphorically, as we can see from Psalm 51. He wrote this Psalm when Nathan, the Prophet, came and fingered him as a criminal and a transgressor of both the moral code of the Ten Commandments and the sex codes of the *mitzvoth*. David wrote

> Have mercy on me, O God, according to your steadfast love;
> According to your abundant mercy, blot out my transgressions.
> Wash me thoroughly from my iniquity.
> Cleanse me from my sin!
> I see that you desire truth in the inward being.
> Create in me a clean heart, O God,
> And renew a right spirit within me
> Cast me not away from your presence
> And take not your holy spirit from me.

In Psalm 32, the theme is continued in relief and thanksgiving after David had come to feel forgiven. There he speaks for all of us.

> Blessed is he whose transgression is forgiven, whose sin is covered.
> Blessed is the man to whom the Lord imputes no iniquity
> And in whose spirit there is no guile.
> I acknowledged my sin to you, and did not hide my iniquity
> I said, "I will confess my transgressions to the Lord";
> Then you forgave the guilt of my sin.
> Be glad in the Lord, and rejoice, O righteous,
> And shout for joy, all you upright in heart.

David was forgiven and God ended up calling him, "A man after my own heart"! (1 Samuel 13:14). Amnon does not seem to have repented, nor does he seem to have experienced forgiveness. He was murdered by his brother Absalom for the rape of Tamar. God instructed Hosea to keep on forgiving his wife, no matter how many times she ran out on him. Moreover, he told Hosea to adopt, as his own, his wife's three children, produced by her adultery and not his kids. God said such forgiveness, goodness, and grace was a model and metaphor of his forgiveness of all humankind. Likewise, the woman caught in adultery and brought to Jesus is not given a chance to speak for herself so we do not know whether she knew how to repent or if she did so. That does not seem to be the issue for Jesus. He simply forgave her outright. She was treated like an object by the religious authorities and only gained any agency over her own life, and any personhood at all, when Jesus addressed her and said, "I do not condemn you. Go your way and don't commit adultery anymore. Don't keep hurting yourself!"

The Bible makes it clear that adultery is bad. In the Deuteronomy sex code it is bad because it violates another man's property. In the Leviticus sex code it is bad because it violates the purity of the woman and the good order of the community. In both records of the Ten Commandments it is bad, as well as in the New Testament references to them. However, there is a very interesting thing about the command forbidding adultery in the Decalogue. The first five commandments are about honoring God and parents. The last five are about contract law. The laws against murder, adultery, theft, perjury, and coveting are laws that spell out the social contract, which is the very minimum necessary to keep a society in good order.

That is, adultery and the other four in this section of the Decalogue are violations of a contract, and that is why adultery is bad. The contract involved is a marriage contract. Many people are quite mixed up about what is correctly called adultery. The only thing that is adultery is having sex with someone when either you or the lover are married to someone else. That is, sex between two persons, neither of whom is married, is never adultery. For sexual relations to be adultery, one of the two must have a contract with a spouse, which is being violated by this sexual tryst.

Many people think that sex between two consenting unmarried adults is adultery. That is not the case. The truth is that the Bible says nothing about sexual relationship between two unmarried adults who have a meaningful friendship but do not intend engagement or marriage. The Bible assumes it is taking place and that it is normal; as natural a thing for humans to do as are any other forms of intimate communication. Some folks confuse adultery with promiscuous sexual relations, that is, sex with or between a series and variety of persons, with none of whom the persons involved have any kind of meaningful relationship. The Bible calls this kind of behavior fornication from the Greek word, porneia. The Bible is against such promiscuousness because it is so psychologically and spiritually destructive. It erodes the personality and the integrity of the personhood of the promiscuous person, but it is not adultery and does not come under that law in the Decalogue.

D. L. Ellens makes the point that while the contract law in the last five regulations of the Decalogue is against depriving a person of his or her guaranteed rights, the surprise in the entire Ten Commandments is that men and women are treated as equals in relationship to the law.[1] Regarding the commandment about adultery, Ellens notes that the primary concern of this command is to protect the woman's sexuality as the property of the man. "Nevertheless, woman . . . is responsible to the law just as the man is. She is moral agent. She is also expected to protect the man's sexual property which, in this case, happens to be coterminous with her body."[2] So, while the woman is somewhat marginalized in this law, and she is an object owned by a man, she is also an agent in her own right, with ability and responsibility to obey the law.

Both men and women are addressed as equal agents with power to act independently, and thus to function responsibly on the own. Children must honor both father and mother. Both sons and daughters, as well as man servants and maid servants, must be compelled to keep the Sabbath. Moreover, when the commandment orders that "*You* shall keep the Sabbath day holy, as well as *your* children and *your* servants of both genders" the reference to "*You*" must be a plural; for if the wife can work then the daughter and maidservant must work on the Sabbath. The plural "You" implies the equality of men and women in and before this set of laws. The relationship of both female and male to the law and to the responsibility to keep it, is the same.

The men are not addressed with instructions for managing the women who would then be spoken about as objects "out there." That is not the case in the Ten Commandments. So the command against adultery is as much a command intended to protect a woman's right to the integrity of her own marriage contract, in terms of her own agency, ownership, and control over it, as it guarantees this right to a man. In this sense too the commandment against adultery is the protection and preservation of a marriage contract, not primarily a commandment about sexuality.

Indeed, adultery is not about sex. The interesting thing is that, while adultery incidentally involves sex, it is first and foremost about breaking a social contract, just as is stealing and murder, perjury and desiring someone else's property for yourself so that he or she cannot have it. Murder is about depriving someone of his or her guaranteed right to life. Perjury is about depriving someone of his or her guaranteed right to the truth. Theft and coveting are about depriving or desiring to deprive someone of his or her guaranteed right to his or her property. Adultery is about depriving someone of his or her guaranteed right to the exclusive intimacy of his or her spouse, as well as of the right to a tranquil home.

When you think of it, these laws were important for any decent and peaceable society. The reason not to steal is because if you have a society in which theft is common you will die. That is, if you steal my TV, you need to stay up all night every night with your shotgun waiting to see what I am coming to take away from you. Thus you get no sleep. You get sick. You die young. That is an unworkable scenario. You want a tranquil life and a stable society? Follow these simply rules for God's proposed kingdom of shalom: peace and prosperity. Do not violate the social contract. Adultery is about violation of the social contract. It will keep you worried and awake nights. Not good for your health! Moreover, it is wrong because it causes a turbulent and unstable society, as does a breach of the other four contract laws in the Decalogue.

There are many reasons people commit adultery. It is quite likely that the reasons are very individual in nature and differ in numerous ways from case to case and situation to situation. However, it appears from the psycho-social research done on these things that there are some consistent, universal, and identifiable patterns which can be described. For many people the most surprising result of research on adultery in Western society was the discovery that it is a misbehavior perpetrated about equally by men and women.

Until the middle of the last century there was a nearly universal belief that almost all men either committed adultery or would like to if they could get away with it; while virtually no women ever did or wanted to. The research of Alfred Kinsey and Shere Hite, cited earlier, blew that naïve and prejudicial notion out of the water. I cannot imagine why that surprised so many people, since adultery between heterosexuals requires a male and a female. Unless one supposed that a few females were servicing the adulterous needs of many more males, an absurdity on the face of it, it would be irrational to assume that there were not as many women involved in adultery as men.

Today, of course, we are much more realistic about women in many ways. That is long overdue. It may be true that during some eras of human history in some cultures, women were more monogamous in nature and behavior than men. This would have related mainly, I suppose, to cultural repression, constraints, and codes. However, that would not mean that women had less internal inclination toward adultery, only less opportunity for it and more overt constraints. Even in the Victorian era of the nineteenth century, when the official codes of social life were rather prudish compared to our day, we now know that a great deal of both adultery and promiscuity marked the lives of a great percentage of both women and men.

Moreover, there is always a tendency in the human community to overlook the fact that adultery is not just a question of whose penis is in whose vagina; or to be politically correct these days, whose vagina is enveloping whose penis. Emotional distraction from a contracted marriage, together with the increased dysfunction in the marriage that that causes, is as much a violation of the contract of marriage as is overt adulterous genital behavior. In fact, one might well speculate that the emotional distraction or attraction focused upon someone other than the spouse, or even upon an idealized fantasy, does more damage to the contracted marriage relationship than adulterous genital behavior. In any case, the emotional distraction is as much a matter of blatant adultery as is the vagina-penis conjunction. That is the point of the remark by Jesus in the Bible, in which he contended that if anyone looks upon someone other than her or his spouse, to lust after that person, she or he has already committed adultery with him or her, in her or his heart.

Limerent addiction is one of the reasons for adultery. Two persons who are thrown into close relationship by a work situation, a team project, a church staff or committee, a corporate management group, a company party, or some kind of entertainment setting like a community bar, a select group of frequently meeting friends, and the like, often sense in each other those unconscious triggers that produce the chemistry of limerence discussed in chapter 4. That happens without warning and is not something one chooses. It is an experience, however, about which one must make a decision about the action to be taken. When both persons experience the same limerent response and find themselves in the agonizing throes of such electric attraction, that situation is a time bomb that must be rather quickly defused or it will lead to explosive expressions of mutual enmeshment and sexual union.

Such limerent relationships are driven with an almost insane, and surely quite irrational force, from encounter to contact to communion, union, ecstasy, and the sense that one has touched the eternal in the exotic experience of this erotic relationship. Rarely do they last through all the pain that the adultery brings into the matrix. Never are they worth the damage done to the marriage contract. The confusion they bring about the true love known in the marriage is immense. The sense of need to have both relationships resolved positively can seldom be met. The ultimate realization that such resolution is never likely, realistic, or humanly possible, leaves one with immense grief and depression. The outcome, whichever way things go from such a limerent relationship, is always filled with somebody's rage, grief, shame, and fear. Limerence is not love and never lasts.

For centuries one of the common explanations for the prominence of adultery in society has been the false notion that men typically have midlife crises at about age 45 to 50 that leads them to seek a new sexual partner. This is a remarkably air-headed and ignorant notion. It is simply not true. There are, of course, men as well as women who are promiscuous all their adult lives to some degree, either in emotional distraction or overt adulterous genital behavior. These are not persons who are simply limerent. They are persons with psychological pathology, whose hinges are rather loose, and who do not generally honor any commitments, contracts, or codes if they can find a way around them. They are the people who, because they are very narcissistic or psychopathic, live their lives with the intention of "always beating the system." These people often fit into the clinical diagnostic category of Borderline Personality Syndrome.

Some similar folks have a perpetual need to lie to themselves, about themselves and about life. They learned at some point as children that they enjoyed lying about things, even when the lie did not gain them anything at all. They are immature and insecure people who cannot be trusted to be forthright and open and honest about anything. They do not know how to be straightforward and how to enjoy the inner pleasure of laying life on the line, so to speak. Such people have no good sense of where the boundaries are between appropriate and inappropriate behavior. They are self-centered, almost always situation inappropriate, impulsive, usually playing around the edges of depression and anxiety, and unable to project themselves into other people's feeling worlds or step outside themselves and see themselves objectively.

They do not realize how disturbed they really are. Their framework of reality does not coincide with reality as normal people experience it. They are certainly Borderline Personality Syndrome as well. We used to call them sociopaths. They do not experience adultery as inappropriate, because the entire world exists out there, in their view, for the purpose of their consumption, use, and gratification. They tend to go from one period of adulterous relationship to another over time and do not feel much fear, guilt, or shame about it. It feels to them like a right that they have, and they find numerous fictional rationales to justify it. This syndrome is equally true of women and men.

However, these are not really the kind of persons who are often referred to as having a male midlife crisis. It is more common than we like to admit that a prominent and highly respected man, like Henry Ford II, Nelson A. Rockefeller, or Bill Clinton, is discovered to have had an adulterous liaison at about age 45 or 50. The easy explanation is always that they are immature men who have experienced a midlife crisis centered around their sexuality. Men, in general, have been severely maligned in this regard. However, after working for 50 years as a clinical psychotherapist, a number of things are clearer to me regarding this issue than they were 50 years ago. Take, for example, the typical case which I now present, documented hundreds of times over in my clinical files. Any thoughtful therapist will recognize the pattern.

A man may marry a woman with the clear and unquestioned sense that the passion he experiences from his bride means that she loves him in exactly the same way and for the same reasons that he loves her. He believes this because her passion and infatuation regarding him looks to him exactly like he feels toward her. He wants to give himself wholly and without reservation to her and he expects that exactly that same thing is what she wants to give to him. As a matter of fact, she may even think so herself, at the conscious level. However, what a man unconsciously needs and wants in marriage is to find in his bride the lost half of himself. He wants to become whole by his union with her. To him it looks like she feels the same.

The reason a man feels this way is that by being born he was thrust out of his mother's womb, where he was totally secure and in total touch with his entire world. Cast out of paradise, he is forever feeling like he has lost half of himself. He tries to hang on to his connection with mother but the stages of life require him to move further and further away from her and become himself, yet he continues to feel that he is only half a self. He tries to please mother, keep her smiling, and measure up to her apparent expectations, but he perpetually fails. She has other children to look after, she encourages him to grow and become independent, every 28 days she does not smile for a week, no matter what he does for her. He fails.

So he finds a girlfriend, buys her flowers, takes her to the prom, courts and woos her, and tries to keep her happy and smiling. He fails for all the reasons he failed with his mother. Things may go well for a while but things change. Life is like that. Then he finds a woman who acts toward him with deep and tender devotion, just like he acts toward her, so far as he can tell. She is just the perfect one. They fall in love and marry. He knows she loves him just as he loves her. He loves her for who she is and for the fact that in her he has finally found his other half, he has become whole.

As the marriage unfolds and children become more of the focus of the family's life, attention shifts. She seems more and more fulfilled as the children arrive. He feels more and more lonely, as both his and her energy necessarily is invested in the children. However, he notices that while he feels he is losing his other half again, she feels like she has finally found her other half. When she was born she was a female, already unconsciously aware that she had a womb and was a life producer. She did not feel like she lost her other half in separation from mother. She is like mother and will find her other half in progeny, the fruit of the womb. What he thought was the same passion for him that he had for her just was not so. She had an unconscious ulterior motive. She loved him because he could fill her womb and so make her whole. He loved her because she could make him whole by being his other half.

That discovery, which usually happens only in bright and intuitive couples or couples in therapy, discloses itself at about age 35. The man continues to devote himself to the family with love and care. Between 39 and 43 years of age, with his wife very interested in him for the quality of life he can provide for the family but not passionate about him as she once was, he finds himself asking, "Is this all there is." If he is a responsible and honorable man, he recommits himself to devoted care of his family and love for his wife. However, he notices that she is less attentive and more preoccupied with some new projects or professional pursuits, since the children are growing and off to school.

At about age 45 he wonders why she is less interested in the sexual communion and more erratic in her moods, just not as joyful, humorful, or playful as she used to be. Then she says her vagina hurts, she does not want intimate relations, she is too busy to go with him to the meetings, parties, family reunions, and church that have been significant parts of their lives. So now they are 50 years old and it is clear to him that whatever else may be said about things, the one clear fact is that he is deeply emotionally deprived. She is in menopause. She was always a gourmet cook, but now their celebrated daily banqueting is suddenly changed. She insists on going vegetarian. The meat, potatoes, and applesauce is obviously gone forever. She lives and works in the house with the lights darkened, when she comes home from work or shopping or her days out with the "girls," as she says. She decides to become a Buddhist. She starts to buy a library of "how to" books on psychology and New Age spirituality. She starts taking classes, the names of which he cannot recognize. She wants to travel by herself, particularly to visit the grown children. "And definitely no sex, dammit," she boldly says.

It dawns on him that her life is full, complete, just as she wants it, without his presence, but on his continuing paycheck. She has launched herself into an alternative world that he cannot understand and in which he may not participate. He is alone, deprived of companionship, intellectual mutuality, emotional tenderness, sexual play, and opportunities for crafting an attractive future with her. He is vulnerable to some kind soul that expresses some decent human warmth and playful optimism about life "as it should be lived." He is in midlife, of course. There is a serious crisis, obviously. But it is not his! He did not cause it. He does not understand it. He is not participating in its dynamics. He is shut out from it. The crisis does not belong to him, nor can he fix it, but he pays an enormous price for it in his sense of abject loss and abandonment. If he is clear-headed at all, it dawns on him that he cannot live in this emotional deprivation indefinitely.

No man wants to dishonor himself, his family, or the wife he loved. No man wants to wreck his estate, his tranquility, his joy in home and castle. But how can he think of living for the next 30 years with death? He did not sign up to live with a corpse in a mortuary, or with a hostile alien in a war. He signed up for finding his other half in a tender connection of mutuality and it has evaporated into thin air because his wife has turned into a narcissistic, moderately depressed, hostile, chronically angry, erratic, independent, alienating, irrational stranger. If he finds love somewhere else, why should anyone be surprised? If in his loss he finds what looks like love and proves to be utter foolishness, who should be held accountable? Is he the one who should be vilified? If he finds himself wishing his wife would catch something and peacefully die, has he become an evil man? He did not ruin the marriage. He did not violate the marriage contract.

For his wife to withhold from the marriage the normal appurtenances of emotional companionship is a violation of that marriage contract. It is an adulterous destruction of the marriage by reason of her selfish distraction to other things, even if that does not involve her interest in another person, though it usually does.

Now, there are some miserable slimy male characters out there who may stand outside the framework of the model I just unfolded, and they probably get what they deserve when their friends flee, the boss frowns, and their caring wives are grossly abused and neglected by them and retaliate. Such characters have their mirror images among women as well. They are a different breed of cat than that which I just described, but these cats are rare.

The most important and interesting thing about all of this, whatever the real dynamics are in any given case, is what Jesus has to say in his discussion of adultery in Matthew 5:31–32; 19:3–9; and Mark 10:2–12. In the last two of these passages, Jesus was confronted with a trick question. The crowds and the leaders had undoubtedly heard him speaking of unconditional love in committed relationships, so they asked him whether, then, divorce was wrong. Jesus' response was that divorce is a bad idea, because trouble in marriage can be forgiven and healed. Then they thought they had him cornered because they had the next question ready. They pointed out to him that Moses, in the law of God, had permitted divorce in cases of adultery, so how could he say divorce was always a bad idea. Jesus' response was both clever and definitive. He said, "Moses allowed you to divorce in cases of adultery because you are so blockheaded" that you cannot forgive. Adultery can be forgiven just as any other sin can be. "Whoever looks upon a person of the opposite gender to lust after him or her, has committed adultery with him or her already in her or his heart" (Matthew 5: 27–28).

Most people claim that Jesus is saying here that lust is as bad as adultery, but that is clearly the wrong way around. Jesus is saying that adultery is no worse than lust and that is the reason that it can be forgiven as readily as any sin, if the person who needs to forgive is godly and not blockheaded like those whom Moses addressed. That is why David could be so thoroughly forgiven that he could write the pathos in that abject confessional poetry of Psalm 51, as well as the poetic expressions of relief and hope in Psalm 32. He was so thoroughly forgiven that he could be called, "A man after God's own heart."

Chapter 10

MONOGAMY: MODELS
AND MEANINGS

The Bible's model of marriage is not monogamy. Most people of today in the Western world are surprised by that, since marriage to only one spouse seems to us to be the established standard. It is the only legal model in most countries in the West. The model for marriage in the Bible is *polygamy,* the term commonly used for what is more correctly called *polygyny,* the practice of a man having numerous wives. Moreover, polygamy is the standard model for a large majority of human beings on this planet. In much of Africa, all of the Islamic countries from the Atlantic Ocean to Indonesia, and Polynesia; indeed, throughout both Eastern and Western Austronesia, marriages are polygamous. This is also true for some regions of Indo-Eurasia, South America, the Arctic, and the like. That was the model in Greco-Roman society too, though the Romans tended to move toward monogamy by the time of Constantine. However, the societies of the Mediterranean Basin, including Jews and Christians, were polygamous throughout the time of the Bible, including the entire New Testament period and well into the age of early Christianity.

The moves made toward monogamy after the close of the NT period, both in the Christian and secular society of the time, were made for practical reasons and not because there was a principle to be followed. Practical reasons for monogamy included economic, social, and psychological considerations. We know that polygamy reigned throughout the NT period because St. Paul wrote to Timothy toward the end of his life and ministry, making a suggestion that officers in the church should probably have only one wife, because of the demands of ministry (1 Timothy 3:2 and 12). Such a leader would be too busy with his commitments to the church of Christ to care for more than one wife, and he would need tranquility at home so he could not afford the risk of unrest between his wives. Paul's counsel to Timothy regarding elders (bishops) and deacons is set in a context describing the necessity for a peaceful and well-regulated home where the church leader has an appropriate setting for study, reflection, and ministry.

Clearly, if Paul needed to make a special emphasis upon and an exception of monogamy for elders and deacons, the prevailing practice certainly must have been polygamy. Moreover, Paul made it quite clear that the reasons for this exception were not principial but practical, as were similar reasons in the secular world when anyone chose to limit himself to only one wife. It is interesting that polyandry is not indicated as common in the ancient world or in the world of the Bible. Polyandry is a situation in which one wife has a number of husbands. This type of arrangement has seldom been seen in the history of the world. There are probably obvious reasons for that. In the ancient world, issues of lineage and inheritance were crucial. A woman with multiple husbands would not likely be sure of the parentage of any child conceived.

Because males throughout history, including today, do not thrive or last as well as females, significantly more male than female fetuses being spontaneously aborted, for example, there are always more females in any society than males. Moreover, in the ancient world death in battle of husbands or potential husbands, death on the hunt, or death from disease tended to be very common. Except for death in childbirth, women tend to live longer than men under any circumstances. Thus, there were many more women in any given society than men, in biblical times and before. As we have noted in a previous chapter, the social welfare and economical solution for that state of affairs was polygamy. This also solved the problem of providing sexual and emotional fulfillment instead of loneliness and isolation for women who otherwise were without partners.

So polygamy was a useful social convention in a society in which war, disease, and other causes of death left an inordinate number of widows and orphans at the mercy of society, where they tended to be exploited, abused, devalued, and manipulated: economically, emotionally, socially, and sexually. This social and psychological problem was radically reduced by the universal convention of polygamy.

Because of the fact that during the time of the rise of NT Christianity the polygamous model in the Greco-Roman world was slowly shifting toward monogamy, it is not surprising that it should also have entered into the thinking of the church community. It is for that cultural reason that it shows up in the late chapters of the Bible, as we have cited. However, there is no biblical foundation for a theology of monogamy. The emphasis of the Bible regarding marriage is, rather, upon its profound meaning rather than upon a specific model or method. Whether monogamous or polygamous, marriage, according to the Bible, must be a relationship of devotion, cherishing, commitment, faithfulness, and enduring love.

Sociologists repeatedly contend that de facto polygamy has always existed in all human societies. Whether that is so is an open question. Research by Alfred Kinsey and Shere Hite, mentioned in chapter 1, would suggest that it is not so, but that experimental promiscuous liaisons have tended to exist for both women and men throughout human society and throughout history. That is not surprising. Humans are not inherently monogamous. The true inner natures of human females and males are polygamous. We all have the capacity to truly love more than one person at a time and to be in love with more than one spouse at a time.

The reason most people in the Western world officially live in monogamy is because that social convention was firmly imposed upon Western society by the Roman Catholic Church in conjunction with the European political rulers of the Holy Roman Empire in the fourteenth century.[1] War and disease had devastated European society so that two-thirds of the population had died. Most families had been bereft of one or both parents. Three hundred thousand homeless orphaned children roamed the cities of Northern Europe. Bands of men looking for work and sexual liaisons wandered the country. Chaos reigned. The religious and political authorities imposed upon the whole society the structure of marriage now known to us in order to create family structures and the stable care of children in well-ordered homes. It was an ingenious solution and it worked fairly well. It was shored up by the papal threat of excommunication and the political threat of imprisonment for anyone who violated this order of things.

In any case, humans are polygamous by nature. We respond with erotic desire to all others who attract us. That is a God-given response. Indeed, it is a stimulating gift. If we do not act upon that desire, it is because we have internalized certain values that discipline our behavior and help us conform to social convention or religious teaching and ethical principles. Undoubtedly, in the early stages of the evolution of the human race, this polygamous eroticism was of great value to the survival of the race. Life was short, everyone was often bereft of his or her beloved, babies often died, and it was important to be able to find multiple partners desirable and fecund. That enabled one to build new relationships and produce new progeny.

Recent experiments in polygamy in the Western world are interesting to study. By the end of World War II, Germany found itself in the desperate situation of having had two generations of men virtually wiped out in World War I and two more generations eliminated in World War II. The consequence was a nation in which there were eight women for every able-bodied man in 1946. The prospects were virtually nonexistent for Germany to be a society based upon well-regulated families, with most of its population coupled and able to produce children. I am told that when the West German Republic was reestablished with its own self-government in 1953, two of the members of parliament were women, and that these two women proposed to legalize polygamy for 20 years. What a good biblical solution to a wretched problem. Of course, the proposal was defeated. Almost all the men voted against it. It is not clear to me if they were voting their conscience or their wives' command. However, it was not proposed again.

A prominent experiment in polygamy was that of the Mormons, who arose in the mid-nineteenth century. Their proposal was grounded upon the same need to care for many women in their society who had been left without a partner because of the death of a husband or for other reasons. They argued for this social solution on biblical grounds, as well, and claimed that it was a religious requirement in their faith. It was their way of obeying the biblical command to care for the fatherless and widows, and the like. Their case eventually was challenged in the U.S. court system and was taken all the way to the Supreme Court of the United States. The legislature and the courts ruled against the Mormons in 1882 and forbade polygamy in the United States.

Unfortunately, both the legislature and the court system claimed that polygamy was against the constitution and, therefore, forbidden. That was an unfortunate development because most thinking and honest people knew at the time that the matter was neither a constitutional issue, nor was it in any way forbidden by the constitution. In fact, forbidding polygamy for Mormons in the United States is a breach of their constitutional rights. It is an infraction of the Bill of Rights provision for the free exercise of religion, as well as a violation of the right to free speech and free assembly. There does not exist in the U.S. Constitution any provision that militates against the practice of polygamy.

One of the more obscene movements against polygamy by Westerners has been the behavior of Christian missionaries over the last couple of centuries. The international missionary movement was particularly strong in the nineteenth century and in the first half of the twentieth. Missions were established in most of what we now call third world countries. These missions have been severely criticized during the last half century for the fact that they intentionally or inadvertently imposed Western culture and values upon the established societies in the countries to which they ministered. This tended to be motivated by misplaced benevolence, as though changing the nature of African societies, for example, to more "civilized" Western ways of life was a gift and benefit to the Africans. There was, of course, no objective basis for forming this judgment. In many cases, this missionary incursion into third world societies produced more destabilization than enhancement. This does not, of course, devalue all the spiritual and psycho-social advantages the missionaries brought to these societies, two of the more prominent of which were education and improved medical attention. But then colonialism was better at both than were Christian missions.

However, one of the most destabilizing influences the missionaries wreaked upon third world societies was the insistence upon monogamy in what had been polygamous cultures. The net result was often that conversion to Christianity meant the disruption of peaceful, established families and the abandonment of former wives to lives of destitution or ignominy. The motivation of the missionaries was grounded in the assumption that monogamy was required by the Bible. How they came to this erroneous notion is beyond comprehension, except that it was the accepted value system in the Western society out of which they had come. They failed to notice the difference between the values of Christianity as rooted in the Bible, and the values of their own home cultures, which, as regards monogamy and polygamy, had nothing whatsoever to do with the Bible.

It is not surprising, in the light of this missionary tradition, that the other monotheistic religion that has invaded Africa and Southeast Asia and that promotes polygamy, namely Islam, has been so well received in the last half century in these third world countries. Why should a man break up his family, disband it as a stabilizing social unit in the society, abandon some of his wives and their children, and adopt a foreign model and mode of life, in order to convert to a religion that champions a merciful God instead of the fearful gods of his ancient tribal traditions? If his options are the disruptive possibility of monogamous Christianity or the congenial alternative of the polygamous Islam, his moral and ethical imperatives are obvious. Islam is the monotheism of choice. Consequently, Christian missions have rethought some of these cross-cultural issues in recent years, but it has clearly been too little too late, most of the time and in most cases.

Islam is growing by leaps and bounds in Africa, despite the strong national Christian churches that have taken root there.

It seems quite clear to most of us in the Western world today that monogamy is the best social convention for marriage in our kind of world. The economic issues of being able to support a family of limited size, the professional issues of many women wishing to have careers as well as families, the emotional issues of handling our proclivity toward jealousy in an increasingly narcissistic culture, and the legal demands of simplifying inheritance rights, militate toward monogamy rather than polygamy. Few women with whom I associate can imagine a household in which they would share the relationship with their husband with other women who would have an equal claim upon him. Men seem even more averse to the idea of being in a relationship of polyandry.

We are acculturated to think of intimate committed relationships as exclusive between two people. Perhaps this is not surprising, in view of the fact that even in the completely polygamous world of the Hebrew Bible, the jealousy between wives in the same patriarchal household seems to have been rampant. Sarah was bitter about Hagar, Leah about Rachel and some of Jacob's concubines, and David's wives could never seem to settle down to a peaceful polygamous household. It is unclear whether it ever worked very well for the women, once their economic, social, psychological, and sexual needs were met.

Polygamy was the biblical model and it seems to have been universal in the Mediterranean Basin and beyond. It was a decent solution to a major social welfare issue; but once women were reasonably taken care of in all those ways in a patriarchal home they seem to have been inclined to bitch and moan rather vociferously about the possibility that one of their colleagues was getting more children, more sex, more attention, more consideration, more status, or the like. Sarah was the one who suggested that, since she was barren, Abraham should take Sarah's servant to wife and bear children with her. When he did, however, it did not take long before she was jealous and had Hagar and her boy, the lovely little Ishmael, thrown out into the barren desert to die. One stands amazed. Jacob loved Rachel. Her father tricked Jacob into marrying Leah, Rachel's elder sister, before he allowed Jacob to take Rachel to wife. The father of the two women, Laban, thought Leah was too unattractive and if he did not marry her off this way, she would never marry.

Leah might have considered herself fortunate. She bore many children and offered her servants as concubines to Jacob. Rachel might have considered herself fortunate because Jacob loved her more, but she was jealous because she seemed unable to bear children, and then finally bore only two, Joseph and Benjamin. Perhaps the polygamous model was a good solution to the welfare problem of care for single women and widows in that society, but one gets the impression from the way many of the named women in the *Hebrew Bible* complained about their status within that system that perhaps it was a good model from the perspective of the leaders of the society who would have had to address the social welfare problems in some other way. The difficulty seems to have been to provide what was missing for the ladies.

Most of the time those leaders were males, definitely patriarchal males. Perhaps this model, despite the fact that it was universal throughout the world at that time and throughout the biblical eras, was considered a good model from the dominant male perspective, primarily. One wonders what the alternative solution would have been. However, had this model not prevailed it is possible that even in those days of limited agency accorded women, the women, out of desperate necessity, would have figured out an idea they would have liked better.

They might have revolutionized society so as to remove the fear and shame associated with singleness, barrenness, and lack of coupling. They might have discovered their identity in becoming chemists and physicists and invented the space age by the time of Jesus. Who can tell what creativity might have been let loose had women been free to think of alternative fruitfulness than sexual effectiveness and progeny?

I cannot imagine my four daughters in a polygamous world, Debbie, a highly productive Hebrew Bible scholar; Jackie, a world-enriching artist and broadcaster; Beckie, an internationally known therapist and teacher; and Brenda, a humorful and hardworking veterinarian. Of course, they spring from a family in which we have thought and talked about these things for half a century, but I fear that had our culture been polygamous when they came along, it would have been hard pressed by them to reconsider some of its fundamental assumptions. I doubt that they would have spent much time bitching and moaning about that polygamous model of the world, but I have the impression that they would have blown it up.

We are all by nature polygamous, but we probably would not do well with it over the long run. One hears stories and reads published accounts of the secret world of the Islamic harems and of Muslim veiled societies. The pictures painted are not pretty. The conditions seem uncongenial to humane treatment of women and to a woman's quest for authentic identity, growth, education, and a fulfilling life of self-determination. The stories that have recently emerged in the U.S. newspapers regarding abuses of polygamy still practiced among certain Mormon families may be exceptions to the rule in that faith community, but those cases seem like horrible caricatures of decent family life or noble, ordered society.

Is it these limitations in the polygamous model that led the rather enlightened Imperial Age of the Roman Empire to move slightly toward monogamy? Is it these impairments of freedom for a full individual life of faith and hope within the community of the people of God that eventually led Christianity to adopt monogamy? Is it the advantages to women that urged the pope and the princes of Europe in the fourteenth century to impose a universal code of irreversible and unbreakable monogamy upon the Western world? If so, that seems to have its virtues. It is not surprising that the cultural code of monogamy has not done very well in suppressing the innate human proclivity to polygamous urges, and has resulted in a surprising degree of promiscuity and multiple relationships in every human community, but at the official level monogamy seems to have served some beneficial purposes, at least for women, and perhaps for society in general.

Whereas the Bible does not propose the model of monogamy, the biblical message throughout the OT and NT demands humane and grace-filled treatment of all human beings: husbands, wives, children, slaves, and even animals. So it is easy to discern what the primary biblical principles are about how humans should be handled and, therefore, how we should treat each other. The overriding considerations are the following: (1) to honor the personhood of all humans, to ensure the physical and psycho-spiritual wellbeing of everyone, (2) to promote the growth and development of every human being to fulfill the maximum of that potential with which God has invested each of us, (3) to preserve with conscious care the dignity and individuality of every persons, and (4) to cherish all of God's children with the kind of love and grace with which he cherishes us all. "In this is love, not that we loved God but that he loved us ... if God so loved us, we also ought to love one another" (1 John 4:10–11).

That, quite obviously, sets the imperative that women as well as men (1) are to be free agents to pursue their destinies in terms of what makes them maximally creative and joyful, (2) are to be individually celebrated as reflections of the very nature of God, (3) are to be empowered to seek such community and relationship as makes them more gratifyingly and fully themselves, and (4) are to be affirmed in their true identity as reflections of the nature of God and incarnations of God's spirit. The option of singleness, or of monogamy in a cherished wooing and courting marriage, seems like a more likely matrix for the fulfillment of all those imperatives in our culture today than does the ancient patriarchal model of polygamy.

Chapter 11

HOMOSEXUALITY: WHAT DOES THE BIBLE SAY IN THE OLD TESTAMENT?

The message of the Bible on homosexuality is neither clear nor conclusive, though many Bible believers think quite the opposite. The Bible was written over a long period of time in the ancient Israelite world, and in the context of the Canaanite, Babylonian, Greek, and Roman worlds that surrounded the Israelites. Like those other cultures, the Bible makes no distinction between homosexual orientation and homosexual behavior. Evaluating the Bible's outlook on either that orientation or behavior, therefore, is complex; and one can draw only limited and tentative conclusions at best. Moreover, the development of biblical ideas and traditions, of any kind about anything, evolved through a number of stages in Israelite and Christian history. Each stage reflected the outlook of its own cultural moment in history. Each such moment bears the influence of important cultural forces and notions from outside the Bible itself.

A good, honest, and complete evaluation of what the Bible has to say about homosexuality, therefore, clearly requires at least three steps. First, we must look at all of the texts in the Bible that speak of homosexuality or imply something about it. This will include the need to understand the contexts of those texts, as well as the need to work out the meaning of the original Hebrew and Greek language of each of them. Second, we will need to perceive clearly how to interpret those texts in terms of what they were originally intended to say to their ancient audiences. Doing that requires an understanding of what the cultural and historical perspective of those audiences would have been. Third, it will be necessary to develop an authentic psychological and theological picture of how those ancient words to that ancient audience speak to our world today. Our world today is a world in which we have vast new understandings of the chemical, biological, psychological, and spiritual makeup of human beings. These insights and the knowledge they give us about human nature and personality were not known to the people of the world in which the Bible developed and to which it spoke. To be clear and precise in our work on these three steps, we will need to define the essential terms used for homosexual orientation and homosexual behavior in Bible times and in our times.

DEFINITION OF TERMS

Homosexuality is the condition in which the process of growing up, that is, of maturation, does not result in an adult who is sexually oriented toward the opposite sex but toward the same sex as that of the person concerned (Jennings, 1990, p. 529). This orientation is not merely a sexually erotic feeling in a person that causes a longing for another person of the same gender. It is a deeper matter of the very nature of that person and involves the full range of personality needs for communion and union with that other beloved person: needs for love, understanding, nurture, fellowship, companionship, and belonging. E. Mansel Pattison falls very short of the mark at this point, inadequately and imprecisely defining homosexuality merely as a psychological-emotional *erotic* orientation and attraction (Pattison, 1985, p. 319).

Moreover, the difference between heterosexual and homosexual orientation is a line or boundary that is not easily drawn with any kind of sharp precision. Individual humans may be found at any point on the continuum between the two extremes of predominant homosexual or heterosexual orientation and need. Bisexual orientation is apparently a manifest need or potential in some humans, as well. There are some reasons to believe the reports that about 7 percent of American males have clear preferences for homosexual experiences and 2 percent are exclusively homosexual in orientation throughout life. The homosexual community itself is quite certain that the true percentages in society are at least twice that high.

It is important to distinguish between homosexuality as the orientation and condition of personal homosexual identity, on the one hand, and actual homosexual behavior, on the other. It is crucial to make that distinction at this point, since truly developing the right appreciation of what the Bible says about homosexuality requires us to discern whether the scripture intends to comment or lay down the law on either condition or on both of them. Since the Bible texts do not, themselves, clearly distinguish between homosexuality as orientation and homosexuality as overt behavior, it seems necessary for us to judge from the context which of the two is at issue in any text from the Bible that we study for understanding homosexuality in biblical perspective.

This issue becomes the more critical when one considers that some persons with homosexual orientation claim to discipline themselves for moral and religious reasons to behave exclusively heterosexually. Some claim to refrain from sexual behavior altogether. Moreover, there seems some considerable indication that confirmed heterosexual persons behave homosexually under certain circumstances in which opportunities for communion with persons of the opposite gender are not present, as in isolated communities like prisons or harems.

In the light of the evidence about homosexuality that was not available in Bible times but is available today, how shall we determine what sort of thing the Bible was talking about when it referred to homosexuality? Today we have a lot of evidence about the psychological and chemical sources of homosexuality and heterosexuality. Was the Bible speaking of these matters, in view of the fact that its authors had no knowledge of the scientific data? Recent brain tissue studies persuade us that sexual orientation is inborn and preset at conception. It does not sound like the Bible was talking about that kind of thing when it consistently suggested that homosexual persons behave homosexually because they make a conscious evil choice that goes against their own God-given inner structures and damns them to eternal perdition.

Today, in the light of the varieties of socially good behavior and bad behavior in both the heterosexual and homosexual communities, it is important to figure out which of these orientations or behaviors is really being referred to by those scriptures which speak of homosexuality. Is the Bible for or against homosexuality? Is it the orientation that we mentioned with which scripture is concerned, or is it the behavior to which the Bible speaks? Does the Bible express itself regarding homosexual behavior only, or also regarding homosexual orientation and identity? Either or neither? Or was the Bible concerned in its day with something altogether different from what we mean today by homosexuality? Let us invite the Bible to speak for itself.

A SCRIPTURAL SURVEY

The Bible speaks very infrequently of homosexual orientation or behavior. At most, six references are identifiable and in three of those, it is by no means certain that either homosexual orientation or behavior is really the matter in focus and the issue that is negatively judged by the biblical text. Three Old Testament texts and three from the New Testament deserve our attention. They are Genesis 19:1–29, Leviticus 18:22–24, Leviticus 20:13, Romans 1:26–27, 1 Corinthians 6:9–10, and 1 Timothy 1:10. Of these it is unlikely that *homosexual orientation or behavior* is the main matter at issue in the Genesis and Leviticus passages. Moreover, it is doubtful that *homosexual orientation* is addressed in any of the scriptural discussions, though *homosexual behavior* seems certain to be.

THE TORAH OF THE *HEBREW BIBLE*

In Genesis 19:1–29 the story of Sodom and Gomorrah is recounted. The story unfolds in a series of six related narrative elements. First, Lot encounters the two angelic figures at the city gate and offers them the culturally required *hospitality to strangers* that was so crucial and inviolable in ancient Near Eastern cultures. He provides them food and housing. Second, the citizens of Sodom appear and demand of Lot an introduction to the strangers so that they may *know them.* Third, Lot refuses their demands on the ground that the strangers had "come under the shelter of my roof," a formulaic expression describing the kind of situation that set in motion the law of *hospitality to strangers.* Fourth, Lot offers the citizens his two virginal daughters to "do with them as you please." Fifth, the citizens feel insulted by Lot for using their own hospitality law against them, as though he were their judge, and for offering them his daughters as substitutes, and they attack him. Sixth, the angels defend Lot by striking the citizens blind. But let the text speak for itself! Its relevant key verses read as follows.

> The two angels came to Sodom . . . Lot saw them . . . and said, "My lords, turn aside, I pray you to your servant's house and spend the night, and wash your feet; then you may rise up early and go on your way." They said, "No, we will spend the night in the street." But he urged them strongly; so they turned aside to him and entered his house; and he made them a feast, and baked unleavened bread, and they ate. But before they lay down, the men of the city, the men of Sodom, both young and old, all the people to the last man, surrounded the house; and they called to Lot, "Where are the men who came to you tonight? Bring them out to us, that we may *know them.*" Lot went out of the door to the men, shut the door after him, and said "I beg you, my brothers, do not act so wickedly. Behold, I have two daughters who have not known a man; let me bring them out to you, and do to them as you please; only do nothing to these men, for *they have come under the shelter*

of my roof." But they said, "Stand back!" And they said, "This fellow came to sojourn, and he would play the judge! Now we will deal worse with you than with them." Then they pressed hard against the man Lot, and drew near to break the door. But the men put forth their hands and brought Lot into the house to them, and shut the door. And they struck with blindness the men who were at the door of the house, both small and great, so that they wearied themselves groping for the door [emphasis mine]. (Genesis19:1–11)

It is noteworthy that there is no direct reference here to either homosexual orientation or behavior. There is some strong suggestion of sexual misbehavior. There may be some implication of potential bisexual interest. It is much more likely, of course, that Lot is so aware of the homosexual interests of the particular crowd that mobbed his door that he saw them to be of no threat to his daughters and, therefore, intends an ironic insult against them by offering them his daughters, knowing that his daughters would be of no interest to them and therefore would be perfectly safe and in no sense at risk. One must imagine that his doing so incites a general burst of sarcastic laughter among the company of family and friends inside the house, including merriment on the part of his daughters, who understand perfectly well the ironic nature of the insult. Indeed, they may have shared those very sentiments frequently around the family table while discussing the state of cultural values among the citizens of their rather rambunctious and unconventional adopted city, in which they could see no hope for a fulfilling married life at all.

No other explanation seems adequate to account for Lot's otherwise thoughtless and cavalier offer of his daughters. Moreover, this interpretation also accounts adequately for the fact that Lot's offer only incites greater rage and urgency in the crowd outside. They turn violent and attempt to rape Lot, himself, and to break down the door to get at the strangers housed under Lot's roof. At the same time, they demonstrate no interest whatsoever in Lot's daughters. Moreover, the sexual implications in the narrative do not come under any kind of clear-cut judgment in the story itself, either positive or negative, regarding either homosexual or heterosexual behavior. Obviously, sexual behavior of whatever kind is not the point of the story nor does it become any kind of issue here.

Quite plainly, the proscription voiced by the passage, through the judgment Lot pronounces upon and against the citizens, is viewed by Lot himself as a proscription against a breach of the hospitality laws. Though the verb, *know,* clearly implies sexual behavior, and in this case, apparently, abusive homosexual intent on the part of the mob, Lot seems not to care at all about that side of things in the story, neither does the story express any concern or judgment about whether or what kind of sexual behavior is intended. The implied sexual behavior seems not to be the issue at stake here. What is at stake is the inviolable prescription for hospitality to strangers in the social and legal code of the ancient Near East. Therefore, it is thoroughly inappropriate and dishonest to cite this story of Sodom and Gomorrah as the basis for any kind of claim regarding negative judgment in the Bible against homosexual orientation or behavior. This story is not a text about homosexuality and how the Bible judges it.

Leviticus 18:22 is more specific and declares,

> You shall not give any of your children to devote them by fire to Molech, and so profane the name of your God: I am the Lord. You shall not lie with a male as with a woman: it is an abomination. . . . Do not defile yourselves by any of these things, for by all these the nations I am casting out before you defiled themselves; and the land became defiled, so that I punished its iniquity, and the land vomited out its inhabitants. But you shall keep my statutes and my ordinances and do none of these abominations . . . lest the land vomit you out . . . as it vomited out the nation that was before you. . . . I am the Lord your God.

The text clearly forbids some sort of homosexual behavior. However, the scope of that proscription and the motivation behind it is not quite as clear in the text. The entire chapter deals with a long list of commands by God against behavior that leads to ritual uncleanness under the cultic or religious worship code of Israel. The chapter ends with the rationale that for Israel to breach these religious worship laws is to lose her distinctiveness from the Canaanites, her distinctiveness as the people of Yahweh. People of Yahweh do not behave in their worship services like the Canaanites who practice homosexual behavior in their cultic worship.

Leviticus 18 is a veritable catalogue of Egyptian and Canaanite ritual practices involving behavior that, in terms of God's religious prescriptions for Israel's distinctive life and worship, were perversions of the worship liturgies devoted to Yahweh. The chapter opens with a repetitious declaration to Israel that she shall not walk in the *statutes* (regulations) of the Canaanites but in the *statutes* of the Lord. There follows the list of practices that the Egyptians and Canaanites employed in their worship liturgies and other related cultic activity: sexually consorting with relatives, sexually consorting with women during their "menstrual uncleanness," adultery, child sacrifice, homosexual behavior, and bestiality.

There are four reasons repeatedly given for God forbidding these practices. (1) Such behavior compromises Israel's religious and cultural distinctiveness;

(2) It is a perversion of the worship liturgies dedicated to Yahweh; (3) It is, therefore, an abomination; (4) The logic is simple: defiling the worship of Yahweh defiles the People of Yahweh, therefore, such behavior will also defile the Land of Yahweh.[1] The land will "vomit you out when you defile it, as it vomited out the nation that was before you." These four are weighted heavily in the passage by being placed against a very specific backdrop, namely, "I am the Lord your God"! The entire thrust of Leviticus 18 is the emphasis upon Israel's cultic or religious worship and cultural distinctiveness.

The Hebrew word for abomination—*toevah*—is crucially significant here. It is a word derived from the sphere of the religious rituals of the cultures of the Near East. It means "to abhor" something for religious reasons. Idolatry is the chief reference to such abomination in the *Hebrew Bible*. Such scriptures as Deuteronomy 7:25, 27:15, 2 Kings 23:13, Jeremiah 16:18, and Ezekiel 14:6 speak of idols as "an abomination to the Lord your God." Leviticus 18, Deuteronomy 12:29–31, 13:14, 17:4, 18:9, 2 Kings 16:3, 21:2, 2 Chronicles 33:2, Ezekiel 5:9, 11, and Malachi 2:11 refer to idolatrous behavior as an abomination.

In his fine article, "Love and Leviticus, Debating the Bible's Stand on Homosexuality," Alex Markels remarks wisely upon the meaning of this key word, *toevah,* in the *Hebrew Bible.*[2] He points out that *toevah* includes the rules of kosher dietary regulations, planting seeds discreetly in a field, trimming human beards, and various kinds of prohibited sex.

> Appropriate sexual behavior is also delineated: Incest and sex during menstruation—both common fertility rites among Canaanites of the time—are prohibited. And before homosexual intercourse, *toevah* proscribes offering one's children to Molech, a Canaanite deity. In such a context, " 'homosexual' intercourse was just one of a list of cultic practices that should not be imitated," says Rabbi Gershon Steinberg-Caudill, who has searched the Babylonian Talmud for examples of how the ancient rabbis viewed homosexual practice. "The point wasn't narrowly about condemning homosexuality but rather about not engaging in the practices of other religions, which were considered ritually unclean." (p. 42)

That the Hebrew word for abomination is a technical term referring to violation of the standard Yahwistic worship liturgy is especially evident in the passages from Deuteronomy, Ezekiel, and Malachi, and thus they are worth quoting to reinforce the point.

> When the Lord your God cuts off before you the nations whom you go in to dispossess, and you dispossess them and dwell in their land, take heed that

you be not ensnared to follow them, . . . and that you do not inquire about their gods, saying, "How did these nations serve their gods?—that I also may do likewise." You shall not do so to the Lord your God; *for every abominable thing which the Lord hates they have done for their gods;* for they even burn their sons and their daughters in the fire to their gods [emphasis mine]. (Deuteronomy 12:29–31)

If you hear in one of your cities, which the Lord your God gives you to dwell there, that certain base fellows have gone out among you and have drawn away the inhabitants of the city, saying, *"Let us go and serve other gods,"* which you have not known, then you shall inquire and make search and ask diligently; and behold if it be true and certain that *such an abominable thing* has been done among you, you shall surely put the inhabitants of that city to the sword . . . [emphasis mine]. (Deuteronomy 13:12–15a [17:4 is the same narrative expression])

When you come into the land which the Lord your God gives you, you shall not learn to follow the abominable practices of those nations. There shall not be found among you anyone who burns his son or his daughter as an offering, any one who practices divination, a soothsayer, or an augur, or a sorcerer, or a charmer, or a medium, or a wizard, or a necromancer. For *whoever does these things is an abomination to the Lord* . . . [emphasis mine]. (Deuteronomy 18:9–12a)

Wherefore, as I live, says the Lord God, surely, because you have *defiled my sanctuary* with all you detestable things and *with all your abominations,* therefore I will cut you down . . . [emphasis mine]. (Ezekiel 5:11)

Judah has been faithless, and *abomination* has been committed in Israel and in Jerusalem; for Judah has *profaned the sanctuary of the Lord,* which he loves . . . [emphasis mine]. (Malachi 2:11)

"Included as an abomination was not only the explicit practice of idolatry, however, but anything that even remotely pertained to it, like the eating of unclean animals and other unclean food (Lev. 11, Deut. 14:3–21)" (Kosnik et al., 1977, p. 189). The assessment of Leviticus 18 for implications regarding homosexual orientation or behavior, therefore, hinges upon the precise intent of that word for abomination, in verse 22 and 29. That is, this statement forbidding homosexuality as an abomination intends to convey the meaning that such behavior, when practiced as the Canaanites practiced it, namely by heterosexual persons in worship liturgies, was, like idolatry, a bad mode of worship, that is, an abomination. It was bad worship liturgy. Not Yahweh's kind of worship service or communal behavior.

This perspective, that the sin is in the violation of the Yahwistic worship practices, is particularly reinforced by four additional Old Testament passages. Deuteronomy 22:5 on liturgical transvestism, and 23:17; as well as 1 Kings 14:24 and 15:12 on male cult prostitution in Israel should be treated in detail, as well. The first passage simply forbids transvestism for men and women. The last reports King Asa's liturgical reforms in which he banished sodomy as a worship practice, which the Israelites had adopted from the Canaanites.

> There shall be no *cult prostitution* of the daughters of Israel, neither shall there be a cult prostitute of the sons of Israel. You shall not bring the hire of a harlot or the wages of a dog into the house of the Lord your God in payment for any vow; for both of these are an *abomination* to the Lord your God [emphasis mine]. (Deuteronomy 23:17–18)
> . . . there were male *cult prostitutes* in the land. They did according to all the *abominations* of the nations which the Lord drove out before the people of Israel [emphasis mine]. (1 Kings 14:24)

These passages illustrate further the forbidden nature of cultic or religious sexual behavior in worship, addressed in Leviticus and echoed in Romans and Corinthians. However the latter three add little new or significant information, perspective, or emphasis to what has been stated already regarding homosexuality in biblical perspective.

In Leviticus 20 we have, quite curiously, a virtual repetition of Leviticus 18. Only two additions are made. First, all the forbidden behavior is described metaphorically as whoredom with Molech, that is, having specifically to do with that Canaanite form of religious worship. Second, the death penalty is added to all of the forbidden conduct including homosexual behavior. Leviticus 20, therefore, contributes nothing to the discussion except to reinforce the link between homosexual behavior and worship misbehavior. It accomplishes this reinforcement by the use of sexual metaphor to describe "heathen" worship practices. Worshipping false gods or worshipping God in a false way, is whoredom, according to these ancient scriptures.

HOMOSEXUALITY: NATURE OR AGAINST NATURE? OLD TESTAMENT MEANINGS

A determination of the precise meaning of the six scriptures studied above depends upon the connotation as well as the denotation of the two technical terms in biblical usage referred to above: the *Hebrew Bible*'s words for "to know" and for "abomination." In addition, accurate interpretation of those scriptures requires a determination of the extent to which some or all of them depend upon mythical apocryphal sources and other influences from the cultural and historical setting that formed the matrix that shaped the meaning of these terms. Let us look at that carefully.

Genesis 4:1 declares that after the expulsion from the garden "Adam *knew* his wife, Eve, and she conceived and bore Cain." [Emphasis mine]. This use of "to know" is a euphemism, that is, a nice way of speaking of the act of sexual intercourse. Such a nice way of saying private or embarrassing things is called a circumlocution, saying it by talking around it rather than just blurting out the truth of it. The term, "to know," was used for marital and nonmarital sexual relations. This use of "to know" functions similarly in the biblical literature to that of the Hebrew verb "to come into" someone, as is evident in Genesis 38:1–30. There we read,

> Judah saw the daughter of a certain Canaanite whose name was Shua; he married her and *went in to* her, and she conceived and bore a son, and he called his name Er . . . Judah took a wife for Er . . . and her name was Tamar. But Er . . . was wicked in the sight of the Lord; and the Lord slew him . . . So Tamar went and dwelt in her father's house . . . In the course of time the wife of Judah . . . died. When Tamar was told, "Your father-in-law is going up to Timnah to shear his sheep," she . . . put on a veil . . . and sat . . . on the road to Timnah . . . When Judah saw her, he thought her to be a harlot . . . He went over to her at the road side and said, "Come, let me *come in to* you," for he did not know that she was his daughter-in-law . . . So . . . he *went in to* her, and she conceived by him [emphasis mine].

Such usage is not confined to Hebrew but appears in other related ancient languages such as Akkadian, with reference to coitus, sexual relations, of both humans and animals (Speiser, 1964, p. 31).

When in Genesis 19, therefore, one finds the term "to know," there seems no good reason for any other interpretation than that of intended sexual intercourse, or sexual relations of some sort.

> the men of the city . . . surrounded the house; and they called to Lot, "Where are the men who came to you tonight? Bring them out to us, that we may know them." (19:4–5)

The interpretation is confirmed by Lot's ironic suggestion regarding his daughters.

> Behold, I have two daughters who have not known a man; let me bring them out to you, and do to them as you please; only do nothing to these men, for they have come under the shelter of my roof. (19:8)

So we must take Genesis 19:4–8 as a reference to intended homosexual promiscuity in Sodom. That such homosexuality is not, however, the abomination for which Sodom was destroyed is indicated by two facts. First, neither the angels nor Lot make a negative judgment regarding the sexual intent or actions of the mob, that is, the narrative does not address their homosexuality as a moral issue. Second, the moral claims made in the pericope have exclusively to do with the prescriptions of the hospitality code, grounded in Lot's argument that the strangers, the angels, had come under his roof and thus he was responsible for their health and welfare, at all cost. The mob's wish is to exploit the strangers against their will. This the narrative harshly judges. Such behavior would breech the prescriptions for proper hospitality current in that culture and essential to its stability. From Lot's perspective, heterosexual and homosexual promiscuity were accepted cultural features in Sodom, but inhospitality to strangers, male or female, by exploiting them without their consent, was severely censurable.

There is no surprise in the fact, therefore, that no tradition prior to the first century C.E. identifies the sin or abomination of Sodom as homosexual behavior. Isaiah (3:9) emphasizes that Sodom's sin was a brazen and unapologetic lack of justice. "Their partiality witnesses against them; they proclaim their sin like Sodom; they do not hide it." Jeremiah (23:14) refers to it as adultery, lying, and an unrepentant attitude:

> In the prophets of Jerusalem I have seen a horrible thing: they commit adultery and walk in lies; they strengthen the hands of evildoers, so that no one turns from his wickedness; all of them have become like Sodom to me, and its inhabitants like Gomorrah.

Ezekiel (16:48–50) speaks of the sin of Sodom as promiscuity, pride, materialism, prosperous ease, and a failure to care for the needy, that is, to give the required hospitality to strangers (Speiser, 1964, p. 142, Kosnik, 1977, pp. 191–192). Ezekiel has the Lord speaking metaphorically to Israel, particularly the city of Jerusalem, as follows:

> You ... played the harlot. ... As I live, says the Lord God, your sister Sodom and her daughters have not done as you and your daughters have done. Behold, this was the guilt of your sister Sodom: she and her daughters had pride, surfeit of food, and prosperous ease, but did not aid the poor and needy. They were haughty, and did abominable things before me; therefore I removed them, when I saw it. (16:15, 48–50)

Speiser's observation in this regard is stated in a special comment on the story about Lot and the destruction of Sodom and Gomorrah by fire and brimstone. His discussion is colorful and illuminating, though, in the end he makes the strange mistake that most other interpreters have made. He starts with a response to the biblical report of the annihilation of the two purportedly wicked cities, whose wickedness had become a metaphor and a byword. He says that to judge from the notices in Genesis 13 and 14 about the nature of these two powerful and prosperous cities and their geological setting, namely, in a terrain full of natural bitumen pits, the story of their destruction by fire and brimstone in Genesis 19 is wholly believable.

> A major natural catastrophe must have destroyed the settlements at the southern tip of the Dead Sea some time after the patriarchal period had commenced. This could well have been an earthquake, accompanied perhaps by an eruption of petroleum gases underground. The event could not but be ascribed to the delinquency of the local population. But there was no uniform tradition as regards the nature of the offense. Isaiah stresses lack of justice . . . , Jeremiah cites moral and ethical laxity . . . , and Ezekiel speaks of Sodom's disregard of the needy. (p. 142)

Speiser then implies that while all of these Old Testament references to Sodom fail to claim that homosexuality was Sodom's sin, leading to its destruction, the Genesis 19 account itself specifically claims that "it was the city's sexual depravity, the manifest 'sodomy' of its inhabitants, that provided the sole and self-evident reason for its frightful fate" (p. 142). This is an interesting observation for two reasons. First, the Genesis 19 account specifically does not fix the blame upon homosexuality but upon the failure of the Sodomites to honor the law regarding the required hospitality to strangers, as Ezekiel points out so clearly in Speiser's own reference to that prophet. Second, this is such a typical slippage in scholarly logic, pervasive throughout the recent centuries of study on this matter, that almost all commenters on these passages make this leap into illogic. They should simply pay attention to the text of Genesis 19. The text does not use the Hebrew word for sodomy.

One is compelled to conclude that this slippage is a consequence of lazy thinking, quite unlikely for a scholar like Speiser; or it is an established inner bias on his part which requires him to judge homosexuality in a morally negative way. So he comes to this text with a conscious or unconscious bias against homosexuality and, thus, intentionally or unintentionally reads the text of Genesis 19 through that bias. It appears that this is true of almost all of the scholarship on this passage and its story about Sodom and Gomorrah.

The reason to point this out so carefully in a book like this one lies in the fact that most of us humans come at all biblical texts in just exactly that same way. It is very difficult not to do so. We are usually quite unconscious of our deepest inner biases about things we fear or have not had a chance to think through thoroughly. This book is about thinking these kinds of issues out in detail and looking so carefully at the texts of the Bible themselves that we can march sturdily through and beyond our personal or cultural misconceptions and really see or hear what the text itself says, what it intended, and what it has to say that is useful for our day and time.

D. S. Bailey provides a detailed evaluation of the homosexual interpretation of Sodom's sin in the noncanonical scriptures (Bailey, 1955, pp. 11–25). The apocryphal sources in Wisdom 10:8 and Sirach 16:8 describe Sodom as guilty of folly, insolence, and inhospitality.

When Jesus, in the gospel stories, refers to Sodom's sin, no connection with sexuality is suggested at all, let alone any connection with homosexuality (Luke 17:29).

> There is not the least reason to believe, as a matter either of historical fact or of revealed truth, that the city of Sodom and its neighbors were destroyed because of their homosexual practices. This theory of their fate seems undoubtedly to have originated in a Palestinian Jewish reinterpretation of Genesis 19, and its exponents. (Bailey, 1955, p. 27; see also McNeill, 1976, pp. 42–50)

Of course, there is, nonetheless, the implication of intended sexual abuse in the Sodom story. However, sexual assault and violence, as physical and psycho-spiritual violation, is always wrong, whether it is heterosexual or homosexual. Therefore, even if homosexual assault were condemned in the Sodom story it would not, therefore, follow that homosexual behavior in other circumstances is wrong. However, it is the case, as we have repeatedly seen and adequately described, that the story of Lot's protection of the strangers who came under his roof is not a story in which homosexual assault is the issue at stake, even though that is what is threatened and intended by the mob. Their named sin was the failure to honor the hospitality code.

There is a passage in Judges 19 about hospitality to strangers, which recounts an incident that is in some ways reminiscent of the narrative elements of Genesis 19 and Lot's story. It concerns the Levite whose concubine was sexually violated by the citizens of Gibeah so that she died. It confirms the point we have made about the ancient Near Eastern code of hospitality. The story in Judges 19 has the following elements in common with the Sodom account of Genesis 19: (1) a stranger is "taken in under the roof of" a citizen of Gibeah, (2) the desire of the townsmen "to know" the stranger sexually, and (3) the offer of the stranger's female concubine instead.

> In those days, when there was no king in Israel, a certain Levite was sojourning in the remote parts of the hill country of Ephraim, who took to himself a concubine from Bethlehem in Judah . . . so they went their way . . . and they turned . . . to go in and spend the night at Gibeah. And behold, an old man was coming from his work in the field at evening . . . and he lifted up his eyes, and saw the wayfarer in the open square of the city; and the old man said . . . "Peace be to you; I will care for all your wants; only, do not spend the night in the square." So he brought them into his house . . . and they washed their feet, and ate and drank. As they were making their hearts merry, behold, the men of the city . . . beset the house round about, beating on the door; and they said to the old man . . . "Bring out the man who came into your house, that we may *know* him." And the man . . . said to them, "No . . . do not act so wickedly; seeing that this man has come into my house. . . . Behold, here are my virgin daughter and his concubine; let me bring them out now. Ravish them and do with them what seems good to you; but against this man do not do so vile a thing. But the men would not listen to him. So the man seized his concubine, and put her out to them; and they *knew* her, and abused her all night until the morning. And . . . they let her go. And . . . the woman came and fell down at the door of the man's house where her master was. . . . And her master rose up in the morning, and . . . there was his concubine lying at the door of the house, with her hands on the threshold. He said to her, "Get up, let us be going." But there was no answer. . . . And the Levite . . . said, "I came to Gibeah that belongs to Benjamin . . . and they ravished my concubine, and she is dead [emphasis mine]. (Judges 19:1–20:48)

There is, of course, one crucial difference between the two stories of Lot and the Levite. Lot offered his daughters out of his freedom, as the patriarchal head of his household in which his daughters were his possession, according to the social code of the time. In the story of the stranger and his concubine in Judges 19, the concubine was protected by the hospitality code, as was her master. The concubine, therefore, was offered to the men of the city in breach of the hospitality code. The men of the city also breached it by abusing the concubine, who was supposed to be protected by them as well as the householder, for she had come in under the householder's roof. The essential behavior intended by the wicked crowd in Genesis 19 and Judges 19 is sexual assault. The moral infraction indicated in the stories is breech of the hospitality code by a number of the characters in the story. The condemned behavior in Genesis 19 is only breech of the code and in Judges 19 breech of the code and murder. In Judges 19 ff. the penalty for the breech of the hospitality code and murder by the men of Gibeah is their being put to death.

In the ancient narrative the upshot of this absolutely horrific story is a war in which all of the tribes of ancient Israel marshaled themselves against the men of Gibeah and, indeed, against the entire regional tribe of Benjamin of which Gibeah was a principle city, and they destroyed that entire tribe.

"Both the stories of Sodom and Gibeah deal with sexual violations. But the fact that the sex victim is interchangeable without lessening the repulsion of the biblical authors, shows clearly that it is not homosexuality or heterosexuality that is the primary consideration here, but the violence" and violation of the *stranger who has come under our roof* (Kosnik et al., 1977, p. 191; see also Bailey, 1955, p. 23). "If sexuality is involved in the condemnation it is subordinate to the issues of hospitality and justice" (Kosnik, 1977, p. 191). In both of these stories or cases, "the emphasis falls not on the proposed sexual act *per se,* but on the terrible violation of the customary law of hospitality" (Phillips, 1970, p. 122).

Neither Genesis nor Judges 19 tolerate violence, abuse, or murder but neither do they condemn homosexual orientation or homosexual behavior, in itself. They do not deal with the former at all and deal with the latter only incidentally. However, the link that Philo makes between Sodom and homosexual behavior, reinforced by 2 Enoch 10:4, the Testament of the Twelve Patriarchs, the Testament of Naphtali 3:4–5, the Testament of Benjamin 9:1, and Josephus' Antiquities of the Jews 1:11, 3, apparently resulted in the fact that "by the end of the first century AD [*sic*], the sin of Sodom had become widely identified amongst the Jews with homosexual practices" (Bailey, 1955, p. 23).[3] This apocryphal and cultural-historical influence shaped the perspective on homosexual behavior taken by Paul, Peter, and Jude.

So by the time of Paul and Peter Sodom had become a symbol of the depravity Christians found to be an abomination in Hellenistic culture. Kosnik (1977) and others point out that it is precisely that symbolic role for Sodom, reinterpreted as homosexual misbehavior particularly, that influenced New Testament writers, in their rare references to homosexual behavior, as one among a number of sins. They forbid it as inherently wrong since it represented the typical depravity of the Hellenistic culture from which Christians were called out to be distinctive as *the church,* those called out and set apart for God.

In that regard the ritual and cultic distinctiveness of God's people addressed in Leviticus 18 and 20 is so relevant. Both Leviticus 18:22 and 20:13, which we studied above, inveigh against sexual intercourse between males. In both instances such homosexual behavior is called "abomination." In both passages homosexual behavior is equated in seriousness with adultery, incest, and bestiality; yet there is one distinction in the condemnation of homosexual activity. It is condemned with the formula that always refers to participation in heathen worship ritual, "It is an abomination!" All the others are condemned as depravity, perversions, defilement, and the like. The emphasis is, therefore, not just upon those behaviors which do not conform to the majority of sexual activities. In the case of homosexual behavior the emphasis is consistently upon its being forbidden because it is an activity of heathen worship practices and thus erases the distinctiveness of the worshipping character of the people of Yahweh.

> The difficulty that confronts us with these texts is the question in which distinguishable respects they are normative for us. It is the difficulty we encounter with much of the Old Testament legislation. For there are three aspects to Mosaic regulations: the ceremonial or cultic, the civic, and the ethical. Some maintain that the prohibition of homosexualism (behavior) was instituted because of the cultic practices of Israel's pagan neighbors and was intended to forbid Israel's participation in such heathen worship practices. That male prostitution was practiced among the neighbors of Israel is seen in Deuteronomy 23:17. If this was indeed the intent of the legislation then it is addressed against a specific (cultic) type of homosexualism (behavior), and it may be questioned whether homosexualism in non-cultic (e.g., moral) contexts is condemned by these passages. (Christian Reformed Church, 1973, pp. 617–618)

The use of the term "abomination" throughout the Leviticus passages is the clue to the essentially cultic nature of their forbidding homosexual behavior. Keil and Delitzsch (1951) relate the passages to the Egyptian goat cult. Canaanite literature has a Baal priest enacting Baal's ritual of intercourse with a heifer. Primitive temple prostitution of both sexes was common in the ancient Near East. Leviticus 18 and 20 are against every form of behavior that represents a loss of cultic identity in Israel, as distinctive in the worship of Yahweh, resulting from emulating or copying pagan worship behavior. Kosnik, quoting from Noth (1965, p. 16 and 1967, p. 49), Snaith (1967, p. 126), Schoeps (1962, p. 371), and Cole (1959, pp. 350–351), respectively, makes the telling point that

The fundamental theme of the Levitical Holiness Code is, "Do not defile yourselves," do not make yourselves unclean. Its concern is not ethical, but cultic. Even adultery is forbidden because of ritual impurity (Lev. 18:20). "Leviticus deals almost exclusively with cultic and ritual matters." For Israel of the Old Testament, the worship of Yahweh was unconditionally exclusive. Anything pertaining to the idolatrous cult of Israel's neighbors was an "abomination" that "defiled" an Israelite and rendered him unclean for the cult of Yahweh. The Old Testament law codes, however, "took their origin in a milieu where no sharp distinction was drawn between the cultic and the non-cultic sphere of activity, but where every side of life had its links with cultic celebration." Homosexual activity between men is proscribed in Leviticus for the same reason that it is condemned in Deuteronomy and the Book of Kings. It is an "abomination" because of its connection with the fertility rites of the Canaanites. The condemnation of homosexual activity in Leviticus is not an ethical judgment. (Kosnik, 1977, pp. 189–190)

Snaith nails it down with the incisive summary point. "Homosexuality here is condemned on account of its association with idolatry" (p. 126).

The Old Testament, then, not only fails to forbid homosexual orientation or identity, by virtue of never defining or considering the orientation or tendency, but forbids homosexual behavior only in terms of its negative cultural, cultic-worship, and ritual role in Israel and her neighbors. Moreover, the proscription falls within a context that (1) equates it with intercourse with a woman during menstruation, a regulation not generally considered to be morally binding today, (2) identifies it with compromise of religious worship distinctiveness over against the Canaanites, an issue no longer relevant in the twentieth century, and (3) forbids it in cases of violation of cultural hospitality requirements, a problem hardly relevant to the contemporary question. In addition, the Old Testament stands against every form of behavior that violates another human, a behavior soundly condemned today in Western culture regardless of whether it is sexual and regardless of the gender or orientation of any of the persons involved.

Chapter 12

HOMOSEXUALITY: WHAT DOES THE BIBLE SAY IN THE NEW TESTAMENT?

As we turn to the New Testament we must address what has been considered the classic passage on homosexual behavior, Romans 1:26–27. It is a bit surprising that at the very beginning of his Epistle to the Romans, Paul makes the following rather comprehensive statement about bad behavior of all sorts.

> Ever since the creation of the world his [God's] invisible power and deity has been clearly perceived in the things that have been made [in the created world]. So they [humans] are without excuse; for although they knew God they did not honor him as God, but they became futile in their thinking and their senseless minds were darkened. Claiming to be wise, they became fools, and exchanged the glory of the immortal God for images resembling mortal man or birds or animals or reptiles. Therefore God gave them up in the lusts of their hearts to impurity, to the dishonoring of their bodies among themselves, because they exchanged the truth about God for a lie and worshiped and served the creature rather than the Creator, who is blessed for ever! Amen. *For this reason God gave them up to dishonorable passions. Their women exchanged natural relations for unnatural, and the men likewise gave up natural relations with women and were consumed with passion for one another, men committing shameless acts with men and receiving in their own persons the due penalty for their error.* And since they did not see fit to acknowledge God, God gave them up to a base mind and to improper conduct. They were filled with all manner of wickedness, evil, covetousness, malice. Full of envy, murder, strife, deceit, malignity, they are gossips,

slanderers, haters of God, insolent, haughty, boastful, inventors of evil, dis-
obedient to parents, foolish, faithless, heartless, ruthless. Though they know
God's decree that those who do such things deserve to die, they not only do
them but approve those who practice them. Therefore you have no excuse,
O man, whoever you are, when you judge another; for in passing judgment
upon him you condemn yourself [emphasis mine]. (Romans 1:20–2:1a)

Paul inveighs against unnatural intercourse by women and homosexual
behavior by men. The entire first chapter of Romans has a special structure
that provides an illumining context for this reference to homosexual activity. After the predictable opening greeting, Paul expresses heartfelt concern
for the spiritual welfare of Christians in the city of Rome, acknowledging
his apostleship to *all kinds* of humans. There follows Paul's section on
God's righteousness, which God gives freely to persons of faith and faithfulness. The fourth section describes God's wrath against wickedness. In
this context homosexual behavior comes under judgment, but rather incidentally, as one of the perversions of human relationships that results from
the primary problem of ungodliness.

That real and primary problem, as Paul sees it, is perversion of our relationship with God that arises out of (1) denial of God's self-revelation in
nature, or out of (2) human arrogance, and out of (3) pagan forms of worship such as idolatry. Paul argues that homosexual behavior is a part of
that idolatrous worship behavior and so it is a liturgical perversion and is
destructive to humans because it perverts their worship of and relationship
with God. Here, as in Leviticus, the religious worship practices of heathen
nations that supplant God with "worship of the creature rather than the
creator" are seen by Paul as being attended by ritual homosexual behaviors.
That ritual idolatry and its attendant behavior, ritual homosexual activity,
is a compromise of the distinctive character of the people called to worship
"the creator who is blessed forever." These are the distinctive people of
Yahweh, the Lord God.

The question then is whether homosexual behavior is, in its own right,
to be judged negatively, apart from worship expressions that are part of
the varied forms of idolatry and thus compromise our distinctiveness as
the people of Yahweh. It seems clear that whatever is abhorred in Romans
1:26–27 is that special kind of homosexual behavior that was involved in
pagan worship rituals. At the very least it must be said that it is homosexual *behavior* of this special cultic type, carried out by heterosexuals,
rather than homosexual *orientation,* which is discussed in the Pauline
passage.

Neither the Greco-Roman world, nor the biblical documents specifically, distinguish between homosexual behavior and inner homosexual orientation. There was no understanding, in that age and in that world, of the psychological or genetic condition of heterosexuality or homosexuality as a psychological or biological and hence systemic orientation. This accounts for the fact that the Bible addresses itself consistently to the behavior only. That is particularly evident in those expressions that predominate in the passages that refer to homosexuality, namely, those in which homosexual behavior is said to identify persons with the non-Judaic and non-Christian religious liturgies.

The second Pauline reference with which we must concern ourselves is 1 Corinthians 6:9–10. Here Paul publishes a catalogue of sinners in which he lists homosexuals along with those who are greedy, immoral, idolaters, adulterers, thieves, drunkards, revilers, and robbers. He declares that these people will not inherit the kingdom of God.

> Do you not know that the unrighteous will not inherit the kingdom of God? Do not be deceived; neither the immoral, nor idolaters, nor adulterers, nor homosexuals, nor thieves, nor the greedy, nor drunkards, nor revilers, nor robbers will inherit the kingdom of God. And such were some of you. But you were washed, you were sanctified, you were justified in the name of the Lord Jesus Christ and in the Spirit of our God. . . . The body is not meant for immorality, but for the Lord, and the Lord for the body. . . . Do you not know that your bodies are members of Christ? . . . He who is united to the Lord becomes one spirit with him. . . . Do you not know that your body is a temple of the Holy Spirit within you, which you have from God? You are not your own; you were bought with a price. So glorify God in your body [emphasis mine]. (1 Corinthians 6:9–20)

Paul's address to the Corinthian Church on these matters makes three points regarding homosexual behavior. First, he points to some of the church members as previous practitioners of the pagan activity and, second, he declares them saved, forgiven, and sanctified by God's grace. Third, he emphasizes the sacral and sacred nature of our bodies, and by implication, our sexual behavior. The Pauline assessment places homosexual behavior on a par with other common sins. His point concerns the difference between the customary behavior of the old pagan way and that of the new Christian status of the believers. In this passage there seems to be some indication that homosexual behavior is sinful in its own right, rather than simply being a compromise of worship or liturgical prescriptions caused by reverting to forbidden pagan religious or social, that is, cultic or cultural behavior. If that is the case, this passage is, in that regard, unique in all of the *Holy Bible.*

However, we should not overlook the fact that this emphasis upon the sacral nature of our sexuality intends to point out that, as all of life is a process and posture of worship and celebration of God, homosexual behavior as part of that worshipful life process seems to compromise the distinctiveness of the people of God and the nature of their worship. It seems to Paul to place those who behave as the pagans behave in their worship, namely, homosexually, in the category of pagans rather than in the category of those whose worship of Yahweh has a different quality and character. That distinctive character and quality has to do with the Yahwistic life of worship being focused upon the Creator rather than, as with the pagans, focused upon the creature (Romans 1:25). I take this to mean that Paul thinks that our sexuality, whether homosexual or heterosexual, must be incorporated into our life of worship of Yahweh, that is, wholly integrated into and balanced within our spirituality. This would make sense out of Paul's remark in Romans 12:1–2:

> I appeal to you therefore, brethren, by the mercies of God, to present your bodies as a living sacrifice, holy and acceptable to God, which is your spiritual worship. Do not be conformed to this world, but be transformed by the renewal of your mind, that you may prove what is the will of God, what is good and acceptable and perfect.

Finally, 1 Timothy 1:10 includes a Pauline reference to Sodomites. Though it is impossible, as noted above, to identify the sin of Sodom as homosexual behavior, since it is so clearly a matter of the breach of the code of hospitality to strangers that was at stake in Genesis 19, it is generally assumed that when Paul refers to Sodomites he has followed Philo Judaeus and the Apocrypha in meaning homosexual behavior. the Book of Jubilees, the Testament of the Twelve Patriarchs, the Testament of Naphtali, the Testament of Benjamin, the Second Book of Enoch, and Josephus' Antiquities of the Jews are all books that are related to the Hebrew Bible but are not part of it. All of them suggest that the sin of Sodom was homosexual behavior. That indicates that by Jesus' time, numerous Jewish interpreters held that the sin of Sodom was homosexual behavior

Philo Judaeus (30 B.C.E–50 C.E.) was the first writer to connect Sodom explicitly with homosexual practices (Kosnik et al., 1977, p. 192). Jude 6–7 and 2 Peter 2:4, 6–10 suggest that the sin of Sodom was fornication and "going after strange flesh." In Jude 7, as in the Book of Jubilees, the matter is related to the sin of the angels and daughters of men described in Genesis 6:1–4, in which the "sons of God (angels) make love with the daughters of men," wreaking havoc upon earth as a result.

> When men began to multiply on the face of the ground, and daughters were born to them, the sons of God saw that the daughters of men were fair; and they took to wife such of them as they chose. Then the Lord said, "My spirit shall not abide in man forever, for he is flesh, but his days shall be a hundred and twenty years." The Nephilim were on the earth in those days, and also afterward, when the sons of God came in to the daughters of men, and they bore children to them. These were the mighty men that were of old, the men of renown. The Lord saw that the wickedness of man was great in the earth, and that every imagination of the thoughts of his heart was only evil continually. Then the Lord was sorry that he had made man on the earth, and it grieved him to his heart. (Genesis 6:1–6)

Because the reference in Jude depends upon the mythic apocryphal evidence from which it is borrowed and makes reference to this completely obscure text in Genesis, it is neither relevant to our study nor a trustworthy definition of the sin of Sodom. Jude calls the sin of Sodom the immorality of unnatural lust like that of the angels who had intercourse with human females, using almost the same language for it as does 2 Peter 2:6–10, which refers to "righteous Lot" being "greatly distressed by the licentiousness of the wicked . . . their lawless deeds . . . lust of defiling passion. . . ." The sin of the angels who impregnated human females and caused trouble thereby, was the sin of violation of the boundary between the transcendent, or heavenly world, and the earthly world. Likewise Jude and Peter, together with the story of Lot in Genesis, see the sin of Sodom to be the violation of the boundary set by the law of hospitality to strangers.

While it is fairly clear that both Jude and Peter are speaking negatively of misused sexual passion, they do not mention the question of homosexuality and they do not turn the flank of the Genesis account which clearly contends that the sin of Sodom was the violation of the hospitality code. The fact that the driving force within the citizens of Sodom was their sexual passion does not come up for censure, in its own right, in Genesis. Thus that is not likely to be the focus in Jude and 2 Peter either, particularly not homosexual passion, which they do not mention. So they must not be talking about the sin of inappropriate sexual behavior on the part of the Sodomites but of the fact that their sexual intensity caused them to sin by violating the code of hospitality to strangers.

The question remaining regarding the New Testament literature on homosexual orientation and behavior, therefore, is that concerning the extent to which the behavior is forbidden on the basis of its being inherently immoral or unchristian, in and of itself, apart from the problem of religious worship rituals. To what extent is it forbidden because of its pagan worship and idolatry connection? To what extent is it forbidden, in the two places it is mentioned in the New Testament, because of an erroneous and unfortunate link made between homosexual behavior and the sin and fate of Sodom? To what extent, in the last case, is the link dependent upon an erroneous dependency of Paul, similar to that of Peter and Jude, upon apocryphal sources from the Septuagint, or upon Josephus and Philo Judaeus? Let us, therefore, explore those issues more specifically.

HOMOSEXUALITY: NATURE OR AGAINST NATURE? NEW TESTAMENT MEANINGS

The New Testament passages that address our subject are clearly dependent upon the Old Testament tradition but add a dimension to the matter, largely drawn from sources that were not in the Bible but in documents like 2 Enoch[1] and the Testament of the Twelve Patriarchs.[2] These documents were apparently well known to those who held the *Hebrew Bible* sacred, including the early Christians. It is clear that a basic line of argument in Romans 1:26–27, taken in the light of the entire chapter, is essentially the same as the argument in Leviticus. Various sins and distortions of appropriate human behavior are indicated, including homosexual behavior, and are condemned precisely because they represent a way of life out of keeping with being the people of God. The general thrust of the chapter uses such terms as *wickedness, ungodliness, suppression of the truth, futile thinking, impure hearts, debased minds, degraded bodies,* and *idolatry.* Homosexual behavior is referred to as a degrading passion that exchanges natural behavior for unnatural acts.

It seems clear that Paul means to describe here a general category of ungodliness, the term that introduces this section of his essay (1:18–25). The essay describes this ungodliness as human misconceptions of God's truth, the truth revealed plainly in creation for all to see. The result is worship of the creature rather than the creator. The consequence of this mistake regarding truth, which Paul claims in the next section (1:26–32), is that humans have succumbed to two problems: degrading passions and debased minds. Degrading passions are sexual dysfunctions in which humans "go against their own natures," and debased minds include covetousness, malice, envy, murder, strife, deceit, craftiness, gossip, slander, insolence, haughtiness, boastfulness, disrespect of parents and God, foolishness, faithlessness, heartlessness, and ruthlessness.

Two hundred years before Paul began to write these things, a book called the Testament of the Twelve Patriarchs was written and apparently was still circulating widely during the time of Jesus and of Paul. In two sections or chapters of that book, the Testament of Naphtali 3:4–5 and the Testament of Benjamin 9:1, there are references that seem to have influenced Paul's perspective and that of the Jewish thinking of his day on the matter of homosexual behavior. In Naphtali there is a brief mention of Sodom as a place where its citizens "departed from the order of nature." No further explanation is given as to the way in which they did this, and while there is no reference to sexual behavior of any kind, there seems to be some relationship between this statement and Paul's declaration that homosexuality is a matter of "going against one's own nature."

In the Testament of Benjamin the sin of Sodom is described briefly as general promiscuity and is followed immediately by reference to heterosexual promiscuity, namely, "actions with loose women." As a result of this behavior, Benjamin says that "the kingdom of the Lord will not be among you." Moreover, the Book of Jubilees, also written 200 years before the time of Paul and well known to the writers of the NT, refers in 16:5–6 to the sin of Sodom as polluting the earth with promiscuous behavior.[3] The type of promiscuity is not specified. We have good reason to believe that these apocryphal texts were ringing in Paul's ears as he wrote that homosexual behavior is going against one's own nature and is a behavior that erodes our distinctiveness as the people of God.

Flavius Josephus lived at the time of Jesus and Paul and wrote a number of books, in one of which, Antiquities of the Jews 1:11, 3, he refers to Sodom and its special kind of sin.[4] About that same time, the book of 2 Enoch was circulating in the Jewish community, as well. 2 Enoch 10:4–5 claims that the sin of Sodom was abuse of children by anal intercourse, while Josephus indicates that "the Sodomites saw the young men to be of beautiful countenances, and this to an extraordinary degree . . . and they resolved themselves to enjoy these boys with force and violence." Obviously, both of these authors, contemporaries of Paul, are inclined to see the sin of Sodom to be homosexual abuse of children or boys. In spite of the fact that in Leviticus 19 the sin of Sodom is the violation of the ancient hospitality code of the Near East, it is clear that by the first century C.E., the time of Jesus and Paul, the view of the sin of Sodom was oriented toward sexual behavior that was against nature, abusive of children, and promiscuous; and that it included both homosexual and heterosexual behavior of that sort, representing pagan practice and eroding the distinctive nature of the People of Yahweh.

St. Paul's outlook on these matters conforms exactly to the perspective evident in the religious and historical books circulating at his time, but which were not biblical books. He was more dependent upon the outlook of those books and the way in which they shaped the thought forms of the Jewish culture of his day than he was upon a strict textual interpretation of the references to the sin of Sodom in the Hebrew Bible, the Sacred Scriptures of his day. Nonetheless, he seems more concerned about the behavior he condemns being an erosion of the distinctive character of the People of God than about the inherent nature of homosexual behavior in itself, if carried on in a true and committed love relationship.

There is clearly a distinction that Paul intends between the sexual dysfunctions, on the one hand, which produce "degrading passions having the consequence that those persons receive in their own selves the penalty of their error," and the debased minds, which produce the list of 17 specific sins, on the other. In the former case the language is very much like that which would describe psychopathology: unnatural behavior that has the weight, character, and valence of an *error* and produces a penalty in the perpetrator's inner person. In the latter case the list of *sins* is specifically referred to as *wickedness* and "those that practice such things deserve to die." This contrast seems more than just incidental or accidental. Paul does not say what exactly the penalty is for the error of sexual abnormality, nor does he indicate how it falls upon those with sexual dysfunction, but it is clear that it impacts equally both "women who resort to unnatural intercourse and men who burn with passion for one another and commit shameless acts."

One might conjecture that the behaviors that are common to such women and such men might be oral sex and anal sex. These Paul might have considered unnatural, though they were not so considered in his day nor are they in our day. Indeed, they seem to have been considered two of the natural forms of sexual play throughout Hellenistic culture, and seem to be considered normal range behaviors in ours.

It is possible, of course, that Paul had some kind of anal fixation and therefore refers only to anal sex in both cases and judges it as a degrading passion. My imagination is probably somewhat limited in these matters, but I cannot think of other options that Paul might be denigrating except bestiality, and if that is what he meant one would think he would have spelled it out, as does the Levitical Code, which can be seen shining through from behind Paul's thought and language. What we do know is that Paul speaks against these "unnatural" behaviors because he sees them as consequences of failing to be distinctive worshippers of Yahweh. Pagan people do such things in their worship liturgies. The People of Yahweh do not do them in their liturgies of worship.

When Paul speaks of homosexual behavior he says that because the Hellenistic people worship the creature instead of the Creator, God gave them up to degrading passions, unnatural relations, and shameless acts, and some internal personal penalty for their error. The problem addressed is the experience of disorder in human behavior and the related disorder within the person. The undefined penalty may be confusion of sexual identity; lack of full-fledged psychological health; certainly some spiritual dysfunction, since it compromises one's distinctiveness as an adherent of the cult of Yahweh; or sexual addiction of some sort. Paul refrains from suggesting that the penalty for homosexual behavior is death, as it is for the 17 other sins listed. The penalty is, instead, some internal psycho-spiritual consequence. Since we can see that the apocryphal writings are not far from his mind, we can be sure that he is speaking against those things condemned in such documents, namely, going against nature, sexual abuse of children, and promiscuity. There is nothing here of the language of wickedness, divine punishment, or sinful behavior that is so blatantly expressed in the next section regarding debased minds and their 17 sins, and for which the punishment is the death penalty of Leviticus 20:2–21, 27.

So Paul does not address the issue of homosexual orientation in Romans 1 and he does not list homosexual behavior with the fatal sins of the godless life, deserving of death. Rather, he describes abnormal sexual behaviors in both men and women, heterosexual and homosexual, as human sickness and distortion that goes against one's own nature, and results from subverting the truth of God evident in the creation. Since in the Hellenistic culture the notion of interior sexual orientation was not known or considered, much less the question of whether it was inborn, developmental, or environmentally induced, homosexual behavior was considered to be a practice of heterosexual persons who engaged in it for the sake of cult ritual or for diversion.

Women were seen as filling the role of home manager and bearer of children, not of sexual playmates. Thus pubescent, girlish boys were often taken as sexual playmates by older men. This seems to have been a common practice in addition to cultic homosexual behavior associated with fertility rites and the like. It is certainly the behavior that the writer of 2 Enoch and Josephus, both of whom were contemporaries of Paul, associate with Sodom. That must have been the mindset of the Judaism of Paul's day.

It cannot be determined, therefore, on the basis of Romans 1, that Paul considered all homosexual relationships to be inherently sinful. It must be concluded, however, that this passage argues that homosexual behavior is at least a pathology, distortion, or dysfunction: an abnormality which is against nature. This seems to be associated with a specific unconventionality, namely, an unnatural, burning passion for nonvaginal intercourse, whether heterosexual or homosexual, whether by women or men.

In 1 Corinthians 6:9–10, the situation is quite different than Romans 1, and 1 Timothy 1:10 is similar to it. In the Corinthian passage homosexual behavior is listed in the middle of the catalogue of sins, for which the twice-repeated penalty is failure to inherit the Kingdom of God, namely to lose out on the flourishing reign of God's love and grace in one's life. The total list of sins includes fornication, idolatry, adultery, male prostitution, sodomy, theft, greed, drunkenness, and reviling. The element in common in all of these sins, of course, is promiscuity. The Bible is generally and consistently against promiscuity *(porneia),* usually translated as *fornication.*

However, promiscuity is possible in many ways, all having the same destructive effect of eroding human personality and personhood. For example, one can be promiscuous sexually, intellectually, spiritually, psychologically, and socially. All these loosen the hinges of one's psycho-spiritual identity and erode one's sense of self. All shear off one's authentic inner emotional or psycho-spiritual self from the gymnastics of one's behavior, whether that is sexual behavior, intellectual behavior, social behavior, or spiritual behavior.

Psychologically and spiritually, it is the same function to engage another person in sexual behavior without an authentic inner emotional connectedness, as to engage another person in profound intellectual sharing without having an authentic inner sense of trust and investment in that person based upon some deep shared goals or ideals. The case is the same when you undertake to engage another person in sharing your deepest spiritual experiences without having established an authentic personal relationship.

When a person sits down beside you on a bus and immediately proceeds to "share Jesus" in intensive and extensive detail, that is personality-eroding promiscuity and situation-inappropriateness. It reflects psychopathology in that person. The hinges are too loose. The same must be said for the stranger next to you on an airplane who immediately feels it appropriate to expound Kant's philosophy, or explain his or her intimate personal odyssey in exhausting detail. These are promiscuous behaviors and the Bible is everywhere against them because they are destructive of human personality or manifest considerable inner pathology and distortion, namely, a gross lack of healthy boundaries, impulse control, cognitive reflection, and orientation to the current situation.

In I Corinthians 6:9–10, it is clear that Paul is against this kind of promiscuity. This is particularly evident in his references to fornication, idolatry, adultery, male prostitution, sodomy, and theft. These are behaviors of persons whom we identify psychologically as suffering from a failure to set and maintain appropriate inner boundaries, either because they are suffering from developmental disorders or from inherited Borderline Personality Syndrome. Male prostitutes obviously are promiscuous in the sense that they solicit promiscuously. They have no identified committed allegiance or covenanted relationship with their those they solicit. Sodomites seek out male or female prostitutes for anal intercourse. They are promiscuous in the same manner as their prostitute counterparts. There is reason to believe that what Paul is decrying here is promiscuity, which, as indicated above, the Bible is everywhere against and which is so obviously destructive of human personhood. That would suggest that perhaps this perspective has something to do with what Paul means in his reference in Romans 1 to an internal penalty which is paid within one's person as a consequence of abnormal sexual practices of any kind.

What does this come down to then? In all of these Pauline passages a number of things may be discerned. First, Paul does not condemn homosexual orientation but neither does he approve it. He simply does not know there is such a thing. As the rest of Scripture, his passages offer no treatment of it since it is never identified as a human condition, in the Bible or in the Greco-Roman culture of Paul's day. They did not know about such a thing as inherent homosexual orientation. Second, Paul addresses only homosexual behavior, as do the surprisingly few other relevant scriptural passages, all of which we have discussed. Third, in Romans, Paul treats at least some kinds of homosexual practice, if not all homosexual behavior, as a human disorder like that of women who practice unnatural intercourse, presumably of a heterosexual nature. Fourth, Paul seems concerned about this because such behavior by men and women reflects the pagan worship practices and not Yahweh's liturgies. Incidentally, there is no indication here that Paul knows of a condition such as lesbianism.

Fifth, in this Romans passage Paul does not list homosexual behavior as wickedness nor assign it the death penalty of Leviticus. In 1 Corinthians and 1 Timothy, Paul describes as sinful male prostitution and sodomy, the only forms of homosexual behavior he refers to in these passages, and both of which are forms of promiscuity. He assigns the death penalty to promiscuity, intimacy without a real established relationship. Sixth, in all of these passages Paul speaks of homosexuality in contexts that sound like promiscuous and obsessive behavior and in none does Paul clearly address the possibility of a homosexual relationship within a troth of committed love and "marriage" (See Olthuis, 1975, on troth). The idea does not seem to arise in his mind. Besides the apparent implications of promiscuity in some or all of these Pauline passages, the Corinthian and Timothy references list the homosexual behavior in conjunction with adultery, underlining the illicit and promiscuous character of the aberration. Therefore, it cannot be determined that Paul intended to condemn homosexual behavior within a troth relationship.

Seventh, there is a general structural correspondence of ideas between Old Testament condemnation of homosexual behavior because it is a compromise of Israel's cultic distinctiveness as the people of Yahweh, and the New Testament condemnation of homosexual behavior as a compromise of the distinctiveness of the body of Christ. These two stood in parallel over against the degenerate aspects of the Canaanite and Hellenistic cultures and worship practices, respectively.

> It must be remembered that the New Testament originated in the era of Caligula and Nero. St. Paul was a contemporary of Petronius, whose Satyricon, along with the writings of Juvenal and Martial, presents a lurid description of pagan life in the first century. Prostitution, male as well as female, was rampant. Slaves, men and women, were sold for sex. Pederasty, child molestation, and seduction were commonplace. Dissolute heterosexuals engaged freely in homosexual liaisons for diversion. Violence was coupled with every sort of perversion and possibility of dehumanization. Confronted by such degeneracy, a Hellenistic Jew like Paul could not but be repulsed. (Kosnik et al., 1977, p. 194)

HOMOSEXUALITY TODAY

Having attempted to read the relevant biblical passages in their scriptural and cultural-historical context, what can we say to the twenty-first century about homosexual orientation and behavior, as viewed from a biblical perspective? What are the prohibitions or constraints in the biblical passages, and are they to be universalized to all forms of homosexual behavior, for all times and situations? What about generic psychological conditions, genetic factors, congenital differences in brain tissue structure in the sex-determining centers in the brain, and which produce or shape homosexuality? What about any early childhood environmental factors that might fix sexual orientation precognitively and subvolitionally? Does the Bible provide room for exceptions depending upon the situation? The creation order seems to have been male and female in union, an arrangement in which native and primal human needs are fulfilled in companionship—in experience with an "appropriate helper." What about committed companionship for the homosexual person who was born homosexual and cannot change?

Obviously, homosexual *orientation* cannot be condemned or forbidden on biblical grounds. The Bible does not deal with it, as indicated above. The most one can say in terms of the specific references to homosexual *behavior* in scripture is that the Bible is against promiscuous and corrupting homosexual activities that have a destructive impact upon others or upon one's inner self. The psychological sciences have long since taught us how erosive of healthy and integrated personhood is any promiscuous practice in whatever sphere of human self-expression.

Recent research published in such estimable journals as *Science, Science News,* and *The New England Journal of Medicine* have demonstrated conclusively the inborn nature of homosexuality, as evidenced by tissue studies of the sex orientation–determining facet of the brain. In this regard it is highly informative to take note of the research reports on brain features and genetic factors that are linked to sexual orientation presented in *Science News* in the late twentieth century.[5] St. Paul would have had no notion of these facts, of course.

There is a burgeoning and converging body of empirical evidence that homosexual orientation is as natural for the homosexual person, and as congenitally predetermined (inborn), as heterosexual orientation is for the heterosexual person. That can only mean, then, under the claims of St. Paul's argument, that a homosexual person may not go against his own homosexual nature any more than a heterosexual person may go against his own heterosexual nature. As that picture becomes clearer, as I am sure it will in the next decade, surely the next century, it will become apparent that if Paul's argument in Romans 1 hangs on the notion that it is wrong to go against one's own nature, that cuts both ways and is as solid a warrant for healthy homosexual behavior as for healthy heterosexual behavior. A person of the opposite gender is an unnatural partner for a homosexual person. Paul's condemnation of exchanging the natural for the unnatural raises the issue of authentic personhood as certainly for the homosexual person as for the heterosexual person and inveighs against willful promiscuity and compromise of a person's authentic self, whether homosexual or heterosexual.

Obviously, St. Paul knew nothing of inversion either as an inherited trait or a condition fixed in childhood. . . . Inversion as a constitutional condition is a phenomenon which lies totally outside the biblical perspective and consideration. . . . Until recent findings of medical science and research came to light, inversion lay outside Christian tradition and theological considerations altogether. (Kosnik et al., 1977, pp. 195–196; see also Schoeps, 1962, p. 373)

If this suggests to some that the biblical perspective looks a lot like situational ethics, it should be noted that Jesus made a very large point of situational ethics being the heart of the Christian Way. The Sabbath was made for people and not people for the Sabbath, he thought, and hence the laws regarding it were to be interpreted in ways that would accommodate the reality of human need as it developed with the changes of time and culture. Jesus was a situational ethicist, but a special kind of one. He was a situational ethicist with a very special bias. His bias was that whatever was legitimate behavior had to be healing behavior that enhanced human growth and well-being.

Jesus constantly set aside principle, precedent, and tradition to act in terms of what was healing for a specific person, in a specific situation, at a specific time. Clearly, that was his principle! His forgiveness of the adulterous woman in John 7–8, instead of following the law that required stoning her, is a dramatic case in point. Moreover, the Bible presents numerous exceptions to the most rigid rules. Killing is forbidden in Scripture, but exceptions are made for war, self-defense, and capital punishment. Marriage is a permanent commitment in Scripture, but divorce is provided for, as an exception. Lying and deceit are forbidden, but Rahab and the Hebrew midwives are approved for it.

Some forms of homosexual behavior, at least, are condemned. Are there exceptions? If so, what are they? A heterosexual is advised by Paul that it is better to marry than to lose self-control and be aflame with passion. Surely the homosexual person who is in the comparable circumstance should be encouraged to find the requisite nurture and fulfillment, as well, in a permanent, committed, faithful troth relationship of love and marriage with a homosexual partner, in keeping with his own nature, as Paul prescribes.

It seems quite evident that in Scripture, homosexual behavior is not the natural order of creation. However, that is not the issue. The issue is rather the problem of whether the homosexual person who finds himself or herself in that state, must be deprived of the full-orbed personhood that is afforded and enhanced by sexual communion and the attendant emotional and spiritual nurture, affection, and appreciation. In their pastoral advice,

Kosnik et al. assert that homosexual persons have the same rights to love, intimacy, and relationships, in terms of their native needs, as do heterosexuals. Under the more general rubrics of Christian love, grace, and growth, that would surely seem to be the requirement of the *Holy Bible*.

Insofar as this may be agreed upon, it follows, of course, that homosexual persons are also required to pursue the same relationship ideals as heterosexual persons are ideally committed to observe. The norms for their sexual activity are the same as those for all human ethical life before the face of God and in his way of righteousness and truth, namely, the Christian bias toward what heals and incites growth in ourselves and others. Minimally this means faithful, exclusive, permanent love relationships, requiring the discernment by the homosexual person and by the community as to what is self-liberating, other-enriching, honest, faithful, life-serving, and joyous; as well as what prevents depersonalization, selfishness, dishonesty, promiscuity, harm to society, and demoralization. These differ not at all from the constraints upon heterosexual persons in relationship, even though the latter are often honored more in the breach than in the observance. These are the universal scriptural requirements for wholesome life in and with Christ and his body, the Church, under God's constitution of Shalom, the Decalogue, and *mitzvoth.*

A consequent imperative of this biblical perspective is that the church and secular communities provide for homosexual persons the same rites of passage, rituals of affirmation, and opportunities for status and promotion that heterosexual persons enjoy. This would seem to include at least the liturgies for marriage into wholesome, exclusive, committed love relationships; regular opportunities for professional roles; and ordination into religious ministry.

Just as heterosexual persons are not indiscriminately attracted sexually to all persons of the opposite gender, so homosexual persons are not attracted to all other persons of the same gender. Sexuality in heterosexual and homosexual persons is not so much something a person does, but rather what that person is, by nature. As they mature, homosexual persons realize their sexual orientation, just as heterosexuals do, and they notice that they are sexually attracted to some and not to other members of their own gender. Moreover, their attraction is not just sexual but emotional, aesthetic, affective, intellectual, and romantic, as is the case of heterosexuals. As sexual drives are not the whole of life for the heterosexual person, so also they are not for homosexual persons. They, as all humans, have their spiritual interests, aesthetic interests, professional interests, employment interests, financial interests, social interests, psychological interests, entertainment interests, intellectual interests, and sexual interests. Furthermore, whether heterosexual or homosexual, we know that our orientation is a core part of us, an essential part of our real nature, whether we are in a relationship or not, virgins or not, celibate or not, incapacitated or not, sexually active or not. Homosexual orientation is not defined by what one does but makes up a significant and dynamically creative part of who a homosexual person is. That truth must be honored by all honest persons.

Our culture and our churches must move to the only responsible position on homosexuality, namely, that it is as normal for a homosexual person as heterosexuality is for a heterosexual person, and therefore, homosexuals need and deserve the same prerogatives of affirmation, love, sexual communion, and socio-cultural opportunity as every other human being. Moreover, it is not ethically or morally permissible for them to go against their own homosexual natures, just as St. Paul insists. This grace and goodness that we must afford homosexual persons is now long overdue. Our prejudice against homosexual persons and homosexuality has been a disgraceful abuse, often driving the homosexual person away from mainstream society and into a promiscuous and destructive world of isolation, secrecies, or even the dark shadows of society.

Chapter 13

BAD SEX: INCEST, PEDOPHILIA, BESTIALITY, NECROPHILIA, RAPE, AND SODOMY

There seems to be a general agreement in modern society that sexual intimacy between parents and children or between siblings, as well as child molestation, sex with animals, genital contact with dead bodies, and like forms of behavior are always wrong. The Bible agrees. It is against eight kinds of sex: promiscuous sex, incest, pedophilia, bestiality, necrophilia, rape, sodomy, and homosexual behavior by heterosexuals. This last one we dealt with in chapters 11–12. As we have already discussed in chapter 9, the Bible is also against adultery. Adultery involves sexual behavior, though that is not its primary violation of the biblical code, as we have seen. Adultery is bad because it is a breech of contract law.

These forms of bad sex are identified in the Bible as aberrant forms of human conduct, gross forms of evil. I believe it is generally understood, today, in Western society, that most of these behaviors are not only specifically forbidden throughout the biblical literature, but that they are clearly understood to be sick, psychologically and spiritually. These are diagnosable psychological disorders, in the codes of the medical diagnostic manuals such as the Diagnostic and Statistical Manual of Mental Disorders (DSM) III and IV. While such behavior was not universally forbidden in the ancient societies surrounding that Israelite community out of which the Bible came, the Bible itself is uncompromising in forbidding these sick behaviors, from the earliest stages of the development of the biblical narratives.

Incest, or sexual relationships within a family other than that between husband and wife, has been taboo—universally forbidden in virtually all known societies from time immemorial. The prohibitions against it have usually been severe. Nonetheless, most counselors, pastors, and therapists are well aware of the fact that incest is surprisingly prevalent in many communities. Anthropologists have invested much research in trying to determine the causes of incest and the reasons for the universal taboos against it. Most of their research results are highly speculative.

However, there seems to be some agreement upon four important points. First, it is generally understood that incest is not only universally condemned but is almost uniformly responded to with a sense of horror. Second, there are rare but well-documented exceptions to the incest taboo, such as the marriage of a prince and princess to preserve a royal line or enhance the awesome sense of divine or religious authority accorded to a monarchy. Third, the variation is surprising from one society to the next, regarding how serious an infraction incest is considered to be, and how intense an emotional reaction and punishment it gives rise to. These levels of response seem to correlate with the frequency of the occurrence of the disorder in a society: the more it is present in a society the worse the penalties are, and vice versa. Fourth, incestuous desires are a very human trait and the environmental situations of life may contribute to whether they are acted out in incestuous behavior or are converted into aversion and taboo.

The theories of Freud, the psychiatrist, and of Emile Durkheim, the sociologist, have been the most influential, in the past, in explaining the causes of viewing incest as horrible. Durkheim thought it had to do with the aversion, indeed the revulsion, most humans feel about shedding the blood of a relative, by accident, violent acts, in war as in cases of civil war, or even by breaking a girl's hymen. Durkheim's notions seem rather far-fetched to most scholars these days. Freud thought that the incest taboo comes from a confluence of mixed emotions about close relatives and strong desires for intimacy with someone of the opposite sex. This, too, seems highly speculative.[1]

From early in the development of the human race, however, families must have noticed that inbreeding, particularly between such close relatives such as siblings or between parent and child, often produced progeny that were severely limited or distorted in their normal functions. Cognitive impairment, susceptibility to certain physical disorders and diseases, and emotional dysfunctions usually limited severely the function in society and the life span of such offspring. This would have led directly to a fear of such phenomena and a tendency to see it as horrid, a horror, and a necessary taboo.

This taboo has had a useful function beyond preventing dysfunctional progeny. It has tended to encourage a wider selection of mates, thus enriching the gene pool in a society, creation of variation in the gene pool by selection of mates from another society at some distance from the home community, and regulating the standards for sexual conduct within extended families, particularly for developing adolescents. That is, the incest taboo contributed strongly to establishing a mutually agreed-upon social order.

Sociologists tend to notice that incest is caused by and causes family stress, strife, and deterioration. A large literature has been generated by them on this matter. The constructive contribution Freud seems to have made in this matter is his suggestion that the Oedipus Complex creates a fundamental psychological conflict that is a foundation stone to the development of religion and culture. In the case of incest, the complex has contributed to the human community's sense of horror at intimacy between family members other than husband and wife, and the translation of that horror into a strong taboo, protecting ourselves against the destructive effects of incest. That is, the Oedipus Complex in this case contributes to the culture by causing us to forbid incest and contributes to religion by prompting us to reinforce that proscription by calling incest immoral and unethical. God is against it, we claim, and so is the Bible. Whether the Oedipus Complex is one dynamic creative force among the normal challenges of childhood maturation, or a terribly destructive force that causes alienation between parents and children, still is not clear to most clinical therapists today.

The essential issues for our purposes, nonetheless, are clear. First, incest is universally destructive wherever it occurs, usually most destructive to the children, male or female; but also enormously destructive to the psyche and spirit of the incestuous parent. This is true whether the incest is acted out in fondling or genital behavior, or insinuated by suggestive gestures, words, postures, or actions. Second, incest is forbidden by the Bible in the most uncompromising terms.

However, as many Bible scholars have pointed out, there is one troublesome thing about the biblical laws against sexual misbehavior, particularly those we studied in chapter 8. Those sex laws in the Leviticus Code and in the Deuteronomy Code forbid all inappropriate sexual behavior between every set of persons that one can imagine in a society, except the relationship between a father and his daughter. Because a daughter was considered to be the property of her father until she was given in marriage, it probably was assumed that no father would damage his own property and her potential for a well-connected marriage. Thus, it is likely that the writers of those sex codes did not feel the necessity to raise this issue as a law. Of course, incest with his daughter would be a stupid and irrational thing for a man to do against himself. And, of course, that is true. But some human beings are just stupid, irrational, and self-destructive enough to commit such incest.

The Bible more than makes up for this lack in the Levitical Sex Texts (LST) and the Deuteronomic Sex Texts (DST) of forbidding incest between fathers and daughters, however, in its ample instructions in both the Old Testament (OT) and New Testament (NT) regarding the care and protection of children and the wholesome treatment of one's family. Paul summarizes this biblical perspective in two epistles and Jesus epitomizes it in one of his most memorable remarks. Paul enjoins us, "Fathers, do not provoke your children to anger, but bring them up in the nurture and instruction of the Lord" (Ephesians 6:4). Again, he says, "Fathers, do not provoke your children, lest they become discouraged" (Colossians 3:21). Jesus declared, "Encourage the little children to come to me and do not obstruct them for to such belongs the kingdom of God" (Matthew 19:14, Mark 10:14). Jesus' classic statement on the matter however, is probably in the following story.

> At that time the disciples came to Jesus, saying, "Who is the greatest in the kingdom of heaven?" And calling to him a child, he put him in the midst of them, and said, "Truly, I say to you, unless you turn and become like children, you will never enter the kingdom of heaven. Whoever humbles himself like this child, he is the greatest in the kingdom of heaven. Whoever receives one such child in my name receives me; but whoever causes one of these little ones who believe in me to stumble, it would be better for him to have a great millstone fastened round his neck and to be drowned in the depth of the sea." (Matthew 18:1–6. See also Luke 17:2, which declares, "It would be better for him if a millstone were hung round his neck and he were cast into the sea, than that he should cause one of these little ones to stumble")

All that I have said about incest applies equally to child molestation. Throughout history the abuse, exploitation, and molesting of children, female and male, has been rampant in all human societies. To think of what dear little children have endured, suffered, and lived with or died from over the centuries is too awful to contemplate and goes far beyond what most of us can readily imagine. Informed estimates suggest that a half million children in the United States are sexually abused each year and another million are physically abused. Moreover, this says nothing about the multitudes that are neglected, undereducated, and treated with only marginal care.

There are numerous accounts of child abuse in the Bible, notably that of Pharaoh attempting to exterminate all Hebrew boys (Exodus 1:16–22), the sacrifice of children on the molten arms of the idol, Molech (Leviticus 18 and 20, 1 Kings 11, 2 Kings 23), and the action of Herod to slaughter the children of Bethlehem under two years of age, generally referred to as "the slaughter of the innocents" (Matthew 2:16). These are all instances of physical abuse and homicide; and they are roundly condemned by the Bible.

Every kind of child abuse is disruptive of the child's normal adaptation to life and his or her healthy pattern of growth. Particularly sexual abuse is enormously disorienting for a child and destructive of that child's personhood and personality. This is even more true in cases in which the sexual molestation takes place before the child has entered puberty. At that point a child cannot grasp what it is that is being done to him or her, since the child has no sense that this is a sexual act. The child can only perceive that it is bizarre, painful, usually secretive and threatening, and out of character for the kind of behavior on the part of that adult that the child expects. Such prepubescent sexual molestation usually results in the development of some form of psychosis in the person molested. Apparently, the experience is so bizarre for the child that it becomes psychologically necessary for him or her to move into an altered state of reality to survive it or integrate it into his or her developing self. Many multiple personality disorders and most anorexia and bulimia occurs in persons who were sexually abused as children.[2]

When the sexual abuse takes place during or after puberty, the psychological damage is usually less severe, more often creating a serious neurosis instead of a psychosis. In any case, the experience always makes it virtually impossible for the molested person to develop any sense of trust, hope, optimism, motivation, faith, or goal achievement.

For example, sexually abused children have a nearly fourfold lifetime risk for psychiatric disorders and a threefold risk for substance abuse. . . . The progression of self-mastery, developmental stages, and relationship with others is altered and disrupted by the abusive experiences. Symptoms such as irritability, school truancy, behavior problems, poor classroom performances, health complaints, sexual promiscuity, running away from home, and lying are common in victimized children. Depression, panic disorders, dissociative disorders, and suicide attempts can also result from chronic abuse.[3]

Two particularly destructive behaviors are typical of sexually abused children, the first in females and the second in males. Sexually abused girls interpret the bizarre invasive manipulation as violence and violation. They conclude correctly that they are being treated like objects rather than persons, since their feelings, emotions, needs, and desires are being ignored. This prompts them to believe that they are not loved by the person from whom they had a right to expect cherishing tenderness.

In consequence, they are motivated by a longing for real love and by rage at the abusing person, to seek attention, love, and sexual certification elsewhere. They pursue every attempt possible to prove that someone will love them and that someone can make them feel that they are still all right sexually, despite the abuse. This produces flagrant promiscuity in most cases, and such girls, molested in puberty or soon thereafter, are usually pregnant at 17 years of age. Now we know why the Bible claims that anyone who causes one of these little ones to stumble like that should have a millstone hung round his or her neck and be cast into the depth of the sea!

Sexually abused boys frequently grow up to be sexual abusers themselves. Apparently they develop the impression that all the usual boundaries have been blown away. Whatever sensations they got from the sexual abuse they experienced, whether by a male or a female, they unconsciously attempt to re-create, probably as a mechanism for healing themselves of the earlier wounding and recertifying that their own sexuality is all right, just as the abused girl attempts to do. Why this creates pedophilia in males and promiscuity in females is not well understood.

> A history of victimization increases the likelihood that someone will become a perpetrator of crime, violence, or abuse. For example, an extremely high percentage of convicted child abusers were themselves abused as children. An important qualification is that victims are not necessarily prone to repeat their own form of victimization. However, there is ample evidence that a victim of childhood abuse is more likely to grow up and victimize others. In the case of childhood sexual abuse, there is some evidence that women who were abused tend to select mates who are likely to abuse them and sexually exploit their children. While these mothers may not abuse their children, they are more likely to marry men who will.[4]

A point of interest that is particularly relevant at the present moment in time has to do with the recent epidemic, indeed plague, of pedophilia cases in the Roman Catholic Church's priesthood. The response of the president of the American Council of Bishops, immediately following the initial exposure of this problem, was to declare on an international television broadcast that this crisis might finally force the church to do something about the dominance of the priesthood by homosexual priests and bishops. This seems now to be followed up in recent weeks with an official announcement from Rome, over the signature of Benedict XVI, that homosexual candidates for the priesthood are now to be weeded out so no homosexual persons will be ordained from now on.

This is of great interest for a number of reasons. The ordained priests of the Roman Catholic Church today, all over the world, include a surprisingly high percentage of homosexual persons. That is as it should be. There should certainly be as high a percentage of homosexual priests in any given faith communion as there are homosexual persons in the general population. This new restriction from the Pope will surely severely reduce the number of available priests in the Roman Catholic Church, which is already unable to assign priests to one-third of its congregations.

However, the other interesting point is the fact that the homosexual priests seem to be taking the fall in this scandal for a disease that has always been seen as a heterosexual disorder, namely pedophilia. This particular form of sexual abuse, pedophilia, is a heterosexual disease in which the normal sexual forces in a heterosexual adult are skewed toward children of either gender, rather than toward another potentially fecund adult. Homosexual behavior, on the other hand, is usually focused upon an adolescent or adult of the same gender.

Perhaps the explanation for this apparent conundrum in the Roman Catholic Church lies in a problem with the data. The media reports upon this epidemic of pedophilia gave the distinct impression that the victims of the pedophile priests were children at the time of their victimization. However, I now understand from a number of informal conversations with priests that the church has done an intensive and extensive research on this matter and discerned that 80 percent of the children who were victimized by the pedophile priests were adolescents at the time of the abuse, and that the abusers were mainly homosexuals.

I find this information hard to believe because it is difficult to understand how the Boston Archdiocese had such a high percentage of homosexual priests that it could have so high a number of pedophiles among its total clergy. If the figures are accurate, Cardinal Law must have been collecting homosexual priests into his Archdiocese with conscious intentionality, in order to get so much higher a proportion of homosexual to heterosexual priests in the Boston environs than exists in the general population. The only other possibility seems to be that his seminary was preferentially selecting homosexual priest candidates into the preordination programs and thus turning out proportionately more homosexual than heterosexual priests. In any case it is curious and the consequences have been tragic.

The generational curse upon families in which child abuse, particularly sexual abuse, has taken place, gives us an entirely new perspective on God's description, in the Ten Commandments, of what happens to those who fail to take seriously and gladly that charter for a peaceful and prosperous society. The consequences of their unfortunate choices will fall upon them unto the third and fourth generations (Exodus 20:5), says the Decalogue. I often hear people denigrating the Decalogue for its negative statements. That is sheer ignorance. The Ten Commandments are positive in the sense that they imply that we may do anything in the world that we want to do except these few constraints spelled out in the commandments, ten such constraints to be exact, which happen to be good for our health and tranquility, our shalom.

Moreover, God does not threaten us in the Decalogue. He simply describes those consequences of misbehavior that are built into the system and from which God cannot rescue us. If you beat your wife for 40 years, you will be a lonely old man. If your wife drinks too much for 40 years you are going to lose her to cirrhosis of the liver. If you sexually abuse your child, you will have grandchildren, great grandchildren, and great, great grandchildren, and so on, who will be distorted by your evil thing, and remember you as the monster that you are. God cannot rescue you from those consequences, even though he can forgive you totally and cherish your children.

God has a preferential option for the children, all the children of the world. Red and yellow, black and white, they are precious in his sight! So we better watch out if we mess with them.

Bestiality is particularly bizarre for most humans to contemplate, yet it is not just a fictional notion. Usually only therapists hear of it, except for those dark-side persons who make a commercial entertainment out of it under the shadow side of the society. It is forbidden by the Bible in the sex codes of Leviticus (18:23–25).

> You shall not lie with any beast and defile yourself with it, neither shall any woman give herself to a beast to lie with it: it is a perversion. Do not defile

yourselves by any of these things, for by all these the nations I am casting out before you defiled themselves; and the land became defiled, so that I punished its iniquity, and the land vomited out its inhabitants.

This law is part of the sex code that includes sacrifice of children by fire to Molech, homosexual behavior by heterosexuals, making love during a woman's menstruation, and adultery with a neighbor's wife, all of which are forbidden expressly because these were the Canaanite nations' practices and eroded the distinctive character and behavior of the people of God.

The research literature indicates that bestiality, the actual preference of sexual relations with animals rather than with a person of the opposite gender, is very rare but is occasionally found in both human males and females. So little is known about the causes, other than a bad habit having been developed, or an extreme sense of inadequacy with persons of the opposite sex, that an insufficient incidence is seen clinically to determine an etiology or a standard treatment. According to the Bible, God knows enough about it to hate it.

Necrophilia is nearly as rare as bestiality. The biblical injunctions against it are similar to those against bestiality. The research literature claims that this illness is more common in males than females, but it is likely that this is speculation based upon the simple fact that a male penis can be forced into a corpse but a comparable female act cannot be made to work similarly. The law against necrophilia is double-barreled in the sense that it is forbidden by the sex code and also by the laws against impurity. Contact with the dead required of the ancient Israelites a specific period of purification under any circumstance. To combine such impurity with intentional genital or sexual interest in a corpse seems doubly abominable to the authors of the Bible.

Rape is understood clinically as an act of violence rather than a sex act. It is usually perpetrated by a male upon a female or another male. However, it is not exclusively a male act. The research literature suggests that more occasions of rape than the public is aware of are perpetrated by women against other women or against males, in which the rapist employs a foreign object or instrument to carry out the violent act. Frequently rape involves genital behavior, and the penis is employed as a weapon in rape, serving more the desire to damage, intimidate, disempower, and inflict pain or punishment than it serves as an instrument for sexual gratification. The sex codes guard women against being forced into sexual activity, but the primary censure against rape in the Bible comes under the larger umbrella of injunctions forbidding violence against any human being or animal.

Finally, the question of whether sodomy is an inappropriate practice is frequently raised today. It has a long history of being forbidden by English Common Law. The name for this behavior derives from the name of the city of Sodom in the Hebrew Bible, as we have already noted above. Such use of the name of that city is caused by a specific interpretation of the narrative about Lot and the men of Sodom. It is clear, as we have seen in previous chapters, that the primary sin of the men of Sodom, against Lot and his friends, was the attempt to violate the law of hospitality. Nonetheless, it is the case, apparently, that the expressed desire of the citizens of Sodom to "know" the two strangers, was a desire to use them as sex objects. From this fact, imaginative biblical interpreters have concluded that the men of Sodom wished to practice anal sex upon the visitors to their city. Sodomy is defined as anal sex.

Most laws against sodomy, namely against the insertion of a penis into the rectum of another human being, male or female, have been removed from the law books in recent years, clearing them from the law codes in American jurisprudence for most states, and also from the codes of most Western countries. The issue at stake here is the problem of identifying the biblical view regarding anal intercourse, on the one hand, and evaluating the appropriateness or moral character of such practice in its own right, as part of the lovemaking play of consenting and committed adults, on the other. Most persons who have thought this through tend to agree that what is practiced, in regard to anal sex, with consent and enjoyment between two consenting adults, in the privacy of their own lovemaking and intimacy, is not forbidden by any biblical code or constrained by an moral limitations. The Bible is against the abuse of another human by the use of the penis as a weapon or tool of degrading force.

So it is clear that the Bible is against bad sex. Incest, pedophilia, bestiality, necrophilia, rape, and so forth are forthrightly condemned by the Bible. They are also considered sick by our current codes of assessing mental health and illness. The men of Sodom were condemned for their strange and potentially destructive behavior, but it is clear that they were condemned for violating the law of hospitality to strangers who had come under Lot's roof, a status in which Near Eastern cultural regulations required the householder to protect the security of the stranger at the risk of his own life. That leaves the issue of anal sex in an ambiguous posture in the Bible. It is overtly condemned in its own right. It is not considered pathological practice in the psychological codes of our day. There seems to be no good reason to censure it if in their own privacy couples find it an enjoyable form of sexual experiment or variation in lovemaking. It does not seem to be the case that the biblical law against anal intercourse applies to our day anymore than does the other biblical sex code law which makes a woman literally the property of her father or her husband, or that which forbids intercourse during menstruation, a time when many women are particularly aroused and free from anxiety about becoming pregnant.

Chapter 14

SEX AND LOVE:
THE REAL THING

In healthy humans sex and love are always intimately connected. That is the way we are wired. God made us that way. There is very good reason to believe that in God the same thing is true. Genesis 1:27, as we have seen, makes it very plain that in some important way God is sexual. He made us like him, male and female. It is not so much that God has some characteristics which are like our sexuality. Rather, our sexuality reflects some fundamental aspect of the nature of God. God's nature is the analogue and our sexuality is the analogy. So we can say, even if we do not completely understand what we are saying, God is sexual.

In exactly the same way, the Bible tells us, God is love. "He who does not love does not know God, for God is love . . .God so loved us, we also ought to love one another" (1 John 4:8–11). It is interesting that Genesis 1 is the beginning of the *Holy Bible* and the epistle of John is nearly the end of it. Here we have the entire book of Sacred Scripture bracketed, so to speak, with these two mysterious statements that define God and define us. God is sexual and he made us like him. God is love and we are by nature the same.

As I said, these two statements are mysterious. In chapter 3 we discussed what it could possibly mean that God is sexual. We thought out a number of interesting and important things that one can say about that. In the end, however, we come away from that discussion feeling that there must be infinitely more about that truth in God than we can possibly fathom. Just exactly what all that means that God created us in God's image, male and female, remains beyond our grasp. We may think it is much easier to know what we are talking about when we say that God is love. After all, we know how to love each other and we feel loved by God in a lot of ways, and so we easily move smoothly over that adage, thinking we comprehend it.

But think of it a moment. The Bible does not just say that God loves us. It says God is love. Just exactly what all that means also remains beyond our grasp, does it not? Of course, so does everything else about God. We can only speak of God in metaphors, after all. St. Paul says, therefore, that now we see reality as puzzling reflections in a mirror and the day has not yet come when we shall see it whole and face to face. Now we know in part. The day will come when we shall know reality as thoroughly as God now knows us (1 Corinthians 13). I assume that means that we shall know the reality of God as well as of ourselves.

So we know God is sexual and we know God is love. We know a lot about what that most likely means but we cannot yet get at the essence of what that means. However, what we can do is realize that sexuality and love are tied together at the center—at God's center and at our center. Sex and love are both expressions of the heart of God. When our expressions of sexuality and of love are genuine and authentic they well up from our hearts and reach out for the hearts of those we embrace.

The biblical concept of sexuality is one in which healthy and wholesome sex is always enmeshed in and an expression of deep and profound committed love. Promiscuity is usually translated into the English word *fornication,* as we have seen. The Bible's notion of fornication is sexual gymnastics with someone with whom we have no emotional connection or commitment. The genuine emotional expressions of our hearts are sheared off from our mere physical sexual gymnastics. Having sex is not making love. The Bible is against this because it is so psychologically and spiritually destructive. It callouses the heart and erodes our capacity to feel truly intimate and connected with the person with whom we are engaging in love play. The Bible affirms the sacred beauty of, and celebrates, sexual play in a substantial and genuinely connected relationship, married or unmarried, so long as neither partner is committed to a different person.

We might spend a moment on that word, callous. All of us get callouses, sooner or later, on our feet, hands, or other places that are constantly rubbed by a foreign object. Callouses are layers of skin tissue that build up on our bodies wherever a sensitive part of us is frequently stimulated with an externally caused sensation. At first the sensitive spot feels a new sensation, if the stimulation continues we feel some irritation, if it is perpetuated we build up the insulating layers of skin that protect us from feeling pain on that spot. A callous has formed and it protects that spot from any injury that might be caused by the constant stimulation. It also renders that spot insensitive. After a while we cannot feel normal sensation at that calloused spot anymore.

In a similar way people who spend their sexual energies merely having sex with playmates with whom they have no heartfelt connection find their souls calloused by these sexual gymnastics and lose their sense of what it means to love and make love. This always happens in lives of promiscuity, but it can also happen in a marriage, if the investment of both partners is not genuinely heartfelt. Then love and sex are sheared off from each other, a thing that happens more often than we would like to believe or admit.

I think sex is like ice cream. By definition, there is no such thing as bad ice cream. There is only good, better, or best ice cream. But if, from neglect, the ice cream melts away, all you have is a mess. Moreover, it is not always possible to clean up the stains. It is always impossible to repair the ice cream; and it is a mess that leaves you grieving and angered about what might have been and now never can be.

To extend that metaphor a bit, you could also say that if a person promiscuously gobbles up enormous amounts of every kind of ice cream without savoring the distinctive flavors of any of it, that person is not only a boorish fool, but he or she will quickly lose the ability to appreciate *any* of it. Her or his taste buds and "palate," as we elegantly say, will be calloused, inured to the possibility of celebrating the true delights of fine ice creams. Is there anyone who cannot get the point of this metaphor? God help you! To shockingly change the image, you might say that promiscuous sex is the hot sauce that a superficial and immature personality spreads over every course of a fine French dinner. Most likely God would not stay around for the meal.

For God and for a genuinely wholesome human being, sex and love go together in an intimate relationship. Surely that suggests that if one is to understand sexuality truly, one must have a fairly profound perception of what love really is. In chapter 4 we distinguished carefully between limerence and love. This distinction seems all the more important when we consider the Bible's great chapter on love. St. Paul wrote it and it was almost certainly one of the earliest formal sermons delivered in the ancient Christian church. It can be found in 1 Corinthians 13 and most of us know it virtually by heart, having repeatedly heard it read at weddings and such celebrations of love. I offer it here in the form of an inclusive language variation on the remarkable translation by J. B. Phillips.[1]

If I were to speak with the combined eloquence of humans and angels I should stir humanity like a fanfare of trumpets or the crashing of cymbals, but unless I had love, I should do nothing more than that. If I had the gift of foretelling the future and had in my mind not only all human knowledge but the secrets of God, and if, in addition, I had that absolute faith which can move mountains, but had no love, I tell you I should amount to nothing at all. If I were to sell all my possessions to feed the hungry and, for my convictions sacrificed myself completely, and yet had no love, I should achieve precisely nothing.

This love of which I speak is slow to lose patience. It looks for a way of being kind and constructive. It is not possessive: it is neither anxious to impress nor does it cherish inflated ideas of its own importance. Love has good manners and does not pursue selfish advantage. It is not touchy. It does not keep account of evil or gloat over the inadequacies of other people. On the contrary, it is glad with all good persons when truth prevails. Love knows no limits to its endurance, no end to its trust, no fading of its hope; it can outlast anything. It is, in fact, the one thing that still stands when everything else has fallen to pieces.

In this life we have three great lasting qualities: faith, hope, and love; and the greatest of these is love. (13:1–8, 13)

So here we have the Bible's poetic celebration of the deep and true nature of this thing called love. Paul's inspired lines are appropriately cast in a kind of lyrical elegy. One cannot read these lines, with an eye for love's truth, without feeling a transcendent connection with the heavenly and the eternal. It would be easy for some to say that this is a far too romanticized picture, painted on a fanciful and ethereal canvas, abstracted far away from the palpable realties we live every day. Can the practical realities of sexual love in the ordinary routines of our daily lives really have those kinds of ideal qualities and dimensions?

Why not? I like Robert Kennedy's attitude at the height of his eloquence. He thought too many people see visions and dream dreams about the ideal possibilities of life and in their lazy mindedness ask, "Why?" He preferred to contemplate the grand opportunities for humanity and ask, "Why not?" Unfortunately, this world could not long endure his large vision and his great heart. But can we not perform well and wisely so central and essential a thing in our lives as sexual love? It is merely a matter of our choosing. Are not our love life and our loved ones worth that sort of extra thoughtfulness and cherishing investment of our real selves that turns mere sex into love and empowers our love for deeply intimate sex?

There are persons, of course, who view sex as merely a genital sensation. Inevitably, they are reduced to experiencing it only that way as well. It must be difficult for such superficial, shallow, and immature persons to bring themselves to imagine, contemplate, or explore deeper connections between sex and love—the kind of deep and enduring, heartfelt love that the Bible describes for us. Their difficulty is deepened by the fact that if one lives sexual life on such a trivial level, it suggests that all of one's life is lived in a way that just skids along the surface of real humanness, real living.

The reason that the Bible can speak so confidently of the enmeshed connection between sex and love lies in the fact that it builds everything upon an ancient Hebrew notion about what humanness really is; and what it means to be a person. The Greek and Roman world of Bible times thought of human beings as made up of body and soul or spirit. They distinguished rather sharply between the functions of each. They tended to think of the body as of lower value than the psyche (spirit, mind, and soul). So the urges of the body were referred to as the lower passions, as though they were only animal instincts. The life of the mind and spirit were thought of as the higher and admirable passions.

As a result, sexual behavior or experience tended to be seen as a lower passion of questionable moral value, to be taken lightly and superficially or to be repressed and devalued. The ideal human was that person who lived in the life of the mind. This sort of schizophrenic attitude toward our sexuality and spirituality is still present in the popular cultures of our world almost everywhere. Some people trivialize sex as merely a selfish entertainment and easily overlook its potential depth of spiritual intimacy. Those who long for and ask for this deeper communion in sexual play are often laughed at and left feeling lonely and very cheap. This makes one feel used and abandoned in the sense that the sexual gymnastics worked but the real love connection did not happen. The Bible is against this. That does not reflect the intimacy of sexuality and love in the nature of God and in the true nature of real humanness.

The ancient Hebrews had a very different view of what a human being really is. They did not consider us to be made up of a body and a psyche or spirit. They saw every human being as a self. To use Freud's term, the Hebrews and, therefore, their sacred book, the Bible, viewed a person as an Ego, a Self. It is this Self that they knew was made in the likeness of God. To be an Ego is to be a unified being. We are not spirits or psyches with bodies to live in. Each of us is a being, an Ego, a Self that is composed of body, mind, soul, and spirit, according to those Sacred Scriptures. You cannot split us up into parts, with each part operating separately from the other parts. We love as selves with bodies, minds, and spirits. We make love with our bodies and minds and spirits, as a unitary self, the lover that relates to another unitary self, the beloved.

So sexual behavior is as much an action of the heart, that is, the inner unseen Self in us, as it is an expression of the body, the outer and visible aspect of the Self. When we shear off sex from love and merely "have sex" instead of "making love," we run a very large risk. We are experiencing what psychologists now call in clinical terms, splitting. It is a fairly serious mental illness with dangerous long-term consequences in the form of important distortions and dysfunctions in our personality formation and expressions. Promiscuous adolescent sexual behavior, for example, often makes it very difficult for the persons who have experimented unwisely with that to develop authentic relationships of intimacy and real love later in adult life. It can take a considerable amount of time and clinical help to heal such a trivialization of one's personality, distorted so badly in the very malleable and formative years of youth.

Splitting is a technical term for conditions in the Ego or the self in which a person's perception of reality is disconnected from reality as it is supposed to be perceived and experienced. Splitting is the experience of acting out a behavior but being unable to feel the normal feelings that are natural to that behavior. Splitting, for example, is involved in a person who can act like he or she is making love but actually does not or cannot feel love; only feels sexual sensation and release. I have counseled persons who have lived and acted in that kind of state for many years and who cannot even imagine, much less recover the ability to experience, love and sex as a unitary experience of their unitary Ego, enmeshed with the cherishing person of the beloved.

Of course, it is also very difficult to find a partner who is not jaded and trivialized by superficial sexual gymnastics and who has never discovered or has long forgotten what it means experientially to realize himself or herself as an Ego in which love and sex are not split. One often hears the adage, "Sex is in the mind." There is a truth to that. Before World War II, a worthy and thoughtful German scholar, Otto Piper, wrote a book, titled, *The Christian Interpretation of Sex.* He revised it in 1960, as the *Biblical View of Sex and Marriage.* He confirms the point we are making here in his clear and simple statement,

> Because sex is a function of man's [human being's] total self, not only of his [or her] sexual organs, a separation between a person and his [or her] sexual nature is impossible. . . . Just as it is not the sexual organs . . . which possess sexual desire, but the Ego or the Self, so sexual desire is not primarily directed toward the sexual organs of another person but toward his [or her] whole person as the bearer of a distinctive sexual character. . . . Although

sexuality is not the only manifestation of the dynamic of the Self it is one of its essential functions. Hence every sexual activity and experience will not only influence one's own *sexuality* but also the *other functions of the self*. . . . Because personal life is indivisible . . . sex must be practiced . . . in such a manner that the other functions of the Self are not disturbed or hampered [emphasis mine].[2]

So it is crucial for responsible and healthy persons to take thoughtful care to make their sexual expressions and relationships more than a passing affair, recognizing that God designed sex and love in such an integrated way that each experience of sexual play and intercourse is designed for and intends to create a lasting union. It is for this reason that we so often notice that in a relationship in which one partner sees the sexual communion merely as casual recreation and sexual gymnastics, the other partner so often feels hurt and used. This feeling of hurt comes from the fact that the person took the sexual play for what it is supposed to be, namely, a union of two persons and two hearts in the deep connection of real cherishing love; only to find out afterward that it did not mean that to the other person. Such an event is sexual abuse of the person who had the legitimate expectations for meaningful lovemaking.

Sex as casual recreation will nearly always leave one of the partners feeling depleted and abused. That is one reason why a meaningful sexual relationship requires a sustained love relationship. Making love is not just "jumping somebody's bones" when the occasion arises, drunk or sober. It is a way of life together. The tender manner in which one lives the whole day, indeed an entire lifetime with the beloved, is the foreplay for the occasions of sexual union. The tone of the way we come and go in each other's lives is a crucial part of the process of making love. It is as much the shared life of the spirit, of the mind, of the soul, as it is of the body. It is the hourly celebration of each other over the days, weeks, months, and years that leads as frequently as possible to the consummation of that ongoing intimacy in the deep visceral connection in which the genitals become the communication line of the endearments of the heart.

That is why the Bible says that each of us is to leave father and mother and lay hold to his or her spouse and thereby become "one flesh," a tangible and palpable unity. Though Jesus did not absolutely forbid divorce, his reason for saying it is generally a bad idea is because it violates that unity. If, of course, that unity was never really achieved, significant therapy is urgently necessary or divorce is almost inevitable. How can one continue to live a lie?

In achieving true union in love and sex some practical suggestions are often helpful. Rosenau and Childerston present the McCluskey lovemaking model that emphasizes the relational and emotional components of life as foreplay.[3] He points out that for meaningful lovemaking four components are necessary: atmosphere, arousal, apex, and afterglow. The elements he thinks are necessary for composing appropriate atmosphere are mature lovers, ongoing emotional intimacy between them, privacy, energy, time, anticipation, initiation of the play by either lover, and mutual consent and desire. Arousal requires that one is open to playful vulnerability, mutual exploration, attention to the senses and the sensuality of the other, and freedom to let the passion build. The apex requires focus on the crescendo of pleasure, offering each other spiritual connectedness, abandoning oneself to the lovemaking, surrender of the self to the process, release of control, and climax. The afterglow is important: returning to the reality around one, cuddling and caressing, affirming each other, sharing reflections and basking in the delight of the experience, and feedback to each other about what made it delightful.

Such delights are possible, I think, only if the daily life of two beloved persons is full of the tenderness of touching, the consolations of good words, the gentleness of kindnesses, and the spirituality of mutual admiration. God is sexual and God is love. That is something of a mystery. He made us with that same mystery at the center. It is possible to plumb its depths and experience its glow. That is what life is mainly about, in God's view, according to the Bible. In that quest we can become our whole selves. Without it we never are.

Chapter 15

SEX AND SHALOM: WHAT GOD HAD IN MIND

When erotic play and sexual union are genuine and truly rewarding for a couple, all of the big problems in life seem like little ones. When the sexual relationship is trivial, shallow, and barren of emotional connectedness, all the little problems of life seem like big ones. We should not be surprised by that. It is the way things are supposed to be. It is clear from the stories about sex in the entire Bible that the appropriate celebration of human sexuality brings a great sense of blessedness and wholeness to human beings; and conversely, the misuse or lack of it brings many forms of disaster: socially, psychologically, and spiritually. That results in an emptiness that causes alienation and loneliness. Loneliness in a relationship is infinitely more painful than loneliness from being alone.

Some of you may glance occasionally at such medical publications as *The Harvard Medical Letter* or *The Mayo Clinic Medical Letter,* the *Journal of the American Medical Association,* or *The New England Journal of Medicine.* If you read such publications or even peruse them occasionally you will have been impressed by the recent research data on how much longer and healthier people live when they have spouses or committed friends than when they are single and alone in their advanced years. You may have noticed informal reports of this research in the daily newspapers or in *Readers Digest.* In any case, the information is quite interesting. As I recall, there is strong indication that people who have lovers, spouses, or committed friends tend to live a decade or more longer than people who do not. Moreover, they tend to enjoy much better health all along the way.

Sometimes, of course, spouses can be a great trial. Some spouses have a knack for taking the beauty and the joy out of absolutely everything. They should be got rid of. Early rather than late! They are a fundamental obstruction to God's intended fruitful shalom in life. They are deadly to all good things in relationship and they will kill you a couple of decades earlier than your normal life span. The stress and anguish they create, put together with the lack of the nurture and delight that you have a right to expect in a coupled relationship, is a killer. They pinch the spirit, quench the joy and vivaciousness of life, corrupt one's dignity and demeanor, undermine hope, distract the mind, and confuse the divine spirit within us. They make wholesome and authentic relationship impossible. They prevent true love and lovemaking from becoming a real cherishing union of God's kind of sexuality and spirituality.

The Bible implies and asserts throughout its 66 books that we are never fully ourselves until we are fully our sexual selves within the embrace of a wholesome and cherishing relationship. The same may be said of the Bible's view of our need to be our true and full spiritual selves. This is an essential part of the great concept of Shalom that dominates the *Hebrew Bible* and is carried over into the New Testament. *Shalom* is a Hebrew word that is also an Arabic expression, *Salaam.* It means the full-orbed and total peace and prosperity in body, mind, and soul that God intends every human being to achieve and enjoy for all of life. It is the ultimate blessing that the Bible declares is God's intent to give to God's entire world for time and eternity.

The Bible is clear on the fact that God brought the world into existence along its precarious evolutionary journey for the purpose of creating us and joining hands with all humans, his co-creators, to fashion a world that would be fruitful in every way. When God speaks in Genesis 1:28 and challenges us to be fruitful, multiply, and replenish the earth, obviously God is urging us to make this universe pay off in every possible way, maximizing all the potential with which God has invested it and us. Fruitful and prosperous, an ideal habitat for humans and all of God's creatures! The ancient symbolic myth of humans in Eden's garden implies that those early biblical authors believed that God intends this world to become a humane home of godlike quality: tranquil, rich, and prosperous in every way in which it has the possibility of growing and blossoming.

What a lovely and challenging vision of ideal human life before the face of God! In this habitat of potential paradise, God fashioned the life-giving bloodstream of sex and love so that every person could become fully human, fully a person, fully a self: whole and healthy in completely gratifying relationships. The design of it all is obviously to ensure that each and every human will become all he or she can be as a sexual-spiritual person.

If you have ever experienced the kind of sex which has linked you genuinely with another human being at the level of your inner self, your spirit, it takes no great imagination to discern the way in which that has the mark of God upon it. It is a gift of unconditional grace. That mark of God can be seen upon the whole created world, of course. We might well call it God's signature, as that of an artist who has just completed a fine painting and with a last touch gives it special identity by affixing a signature.

Three thousand years ago the writer of the biblical Psalms saw this and declared, "O Lord, our Lord, how excellent is thy name in all the earth" (Psalm 8:1). I have often thought that there are those throughout the world who do not exalt the name of God, despite the fact that God's fingerprints are everywhere evident in his created world. Perhaps the Psalmist's words would speak a little more clearly if we recognized that what Psalm 8:1 means to say is really this, "O Lord, our Lord, how excellent is your signature everywhere in this universe."

Moreover, it is clear to see everywhere that the whole world is designed in detail to offer an infinite and inexhaustible resource for enriched human life. We have not been very efficient in using it well over the centuries, in making it pay off for the maximum benefit of all humankind, but that does not take away the fact that the God-given magnificence of this world is remarkably more than what all humankind would need for a nearly perfect world for the body, mind, and spirit. Everywhere God's benevolent signature can be seen.

For example, I am repeatedly impressed by the mindfulness of the universe, the benevolent providence evident in the golden thread of guided development throughout history, the irrepressible urge in all things toward beauty, and the remarkable way in which the biblical assurances of forgiveness and unconditional acceptance by God for every human are tailored exactly for our greatest need. They are obviously designed to deliver us from every form of fear, guilt, and shame. The biblical message clearly declares that God has removed all three of those monsters from the equation of our relationship to God, as well as from our interaction with each other, and with the created world. Moreover, the rich and tasty filling in this marvelous layer cake of divine blessings is the gift of sexuality and love; God's intended kind of meaningful and cherishing sex and love.

That is undoubtedly why the Bible keeps the focus of human sexuality upon the issue of wholesome and truly connected relationships. Only such relationships are the appropriately cherishing setting for sex and lovemaking.

True and wholesome love may be love at first sight or the long-developing love that eventually sneaks up on a couple, so to speak, and surprises them with the realization that they have a special relationship or a special attraction for each other. They are, to their own great surprise, in love.

Whether love springs up suddenly or develops slowly, it may start at the head, the heart, or the crotch. That is, a genuine love relationship may start with meaningful emotional mutuality, or with a surprisingly gratifying intellectual sharing, or with an intense erotic interest in each other. It may be the result of the two persons sensing that they are on the same wavelength, so to speak, in thoughtful interests about enjoyable ideas, stimulating feelings, or genital electricity.

It is usually the case that if a relationship starts at the head it grows natural to a connection of the heart between the two people, and then it eventually involves a physical connection that leads to an erotic genital union. Similarly, if the relationship arises out of the tenderness of gentle feelings of emotional mutuality, it can eventually spread throughout life experiences to include the couple's intellectual sharing and erotic appreciation of each other. It seems apparent from the history of human eroticism, however, that when a relationship starts at the crotch it seldom goes anywhere from there. It tends to stay at the crotch. That should not be a surprise. The electric charge usually generated by genital connection is often so strong that it becomes the entire preoccupation of the relationship and the couple seldom moves out from there to discover each other's emotional and intellectual nature and interests. That leaves them with a very truncated union. Underdeveloped and precarious! Fragile!

Undoubtedly, we can see God's imprint in these facts of life and relationship, as well as in the design of the heavens and the earth to which the Psalmist called our attention. God has wired us in such a way that we are intended for a full-orbed life and full-orbed relationships. We are not wholly ourselves until we are in relationships that are fruitfully connected at the head, heart, and crotch. That very fact, written throughout our very natures as human beings, is God's signature upon us. We do well, I am sure, to take it seriously.

Bible authors, readers, and believers, throughout the centuries have been able to see God's signature in his world and take heart. Undoubtedly that is true of all humans who have held dear their own Sacred Scriptures. The heartening experience in noticing God's fingerprints or signature everywhere in the world comes from the sense of peace and purpose we get when we know clearly that we are in God's caring hands, as well as in God's will and way. When I look at the complexity and order in this grand universe, from the orbiting planets to the subatomic particles, it gives me a deep sense of reassurance that behind this mindful design is an incredibly thoughtful mind. Moreover, it is evident everywhere that this mindful God who stands behind the universe is caring and wise and has an eye for beauty.

When I look back upon the three quarters of a century during which I have been noticing these things, I must confess that God's golden thread of provident guidance in my life astounds me. For 74 years I have worked hard to manhandle into place all those things that I thought were the crucial things that had to be accomplished in my life for it to be responsible, gratifying, and fruitful. As it turns out, those major issues or events that I thought meant everything and needed to be got just right, have for the most part ended up being virtually irrelevant. The things which I thought were terribly unfortunate, which God should have prevented from happening to me at all cost, if he had his head screwed on right, turned out to be the hinges of my destiny. Upon them all the important developments and growth in my life turned.

God's signature is written everywhere across the unfolding pilgrimage of my life, and my fingerprints are mostly just messy smudges along the way. Most thoughtful people will say the same. My life has been full of pain. If you knew all about me you might define it, from one point of view at least, as one long gasp of grief. But the truth about my life is that it has been full of meaning all along the way. Full of God's kind of meaning! Full of shalom. Much of the shalom came from my growth through pain.

Some folks never seem able to see the shalom and they make me wonder whether they are genetically preset to love misery more than wholeness and prosperity of mind and spirit. The Psalmist could not repress his sense of optimism about the beauty of God's fingerprints that he saw everywhere. In Psalm 19 he says it like this, in my rather free translation of the ancient Hebrew.

> The heavens shout out the glory of God
> The sky proclaims his clever work.
> Each day communicates profusely to the next day
> And each night to the next reveals knowledge about God
> There is no real speaking, they do not sound out words
> You cannot hear any voices
> Yet their expressions go out throughout all this planet
> And their messages to the far reaches of this world.

This writer of poetic songs in praise of God has caught the sense of order and beauty in everything and cannot keep quiet. There follows in

this Psalm an exciting description of the majesty of the sun rising and setting, making its way across the sky, warming and quickening everywhere
all life on this planet. Then the Psalmist turns his attention to the beauty of
God's word, the Torah, Israel's most Sacred Scriptures.

> The Word of the Lord is perfect refreshing the soul.
> The testimony of the Lord is trustworthy, making simple ones wise
> The regulations of the Lord make sense, they make the heart sing.
> The commandments of the Lord are right on, opening our eyes.
> To stand in awe of God makes one feel authentic,
>   like you could be real forever.
> The Lord's organization and design of things ring true,
>   just the way things ought to be.
> This setup is worth more than a fortune,
>   more satisfying than a feast with dessert.

David ends this celebrative Psalm about God's shalom with a grateful,
prayerful expostulation:

> O Lord, you are my rock and my redeemer!

NOTES

SERIES FOREWORD

1. L. Aden & J. H. Ellens (1990), *Turning points in pastoral care: The legacy of Anton Boisen and Seward Hiltner,* Grand Rapids, MI: Baker.

FOREWORD

1. Erik H. Erikson (1981), The Galilean sayings and the sense of "I," in *The Yale Review, 70,* 321–362. The quotation is on page 340.

PREFACE

1. J. H. Ellens (2006), *Sex in the Bible,* Westport, CT: Praeger, 210.
2. Ibid., 6.
3. Ibid., 7.
4. P. Hein (1969), *More Grooks,* London: Hodder Paperbacks, 31.

CHAPTER 1

1. A. C. Kinsey (1948), *Sexual behavior in the human male,* Philadelphia: Saunders; A. C. Kinsey (1953), *Sexual behavior in the human female,* Philadelphia: Saunders; Kinsey's two volumes were republished by Indiana University Press in 1998.
2. W. H. Masters & V. E. Johnson (1966), *Human sexual response,* Boston: Little and Brown.
3. S. Hite (1976), *The Hite report,* New York: Macmillan, London: Collier.

CHAPTER 3

1. Jack Miles, in his 1995 Pulitzer Prize winner, *God: A biography,* New York: Knopf, suggests on pages 28–38 that God's unaccountable fury after Adam and Eve ate the forbidden fruit indicates his desire for communion and union with them. Miles suggests that this gives us a clue as to why God created them. He implies, as the ancient Greeks sometimes thought, that this longing for humans within the character of God is the force of God's Eros, the force that produced the entire creation, God's desire to possess the creation as his object. Thus, when Adam and Eve ate the forbidden fruit they expressed independence, jeopardizing God's erotic love for them. Or it expresses the force of filial love in God, his desire to have humans as his companions, being thus infuriated when in his wooing them he loses out to their erotic discovery of and hence preoccupation with each other.

CHAPTER 4

1. P. Gray (1993, February 15), What is love?, *Time, 49* (3), 47.
2. S. Massie (1980), *Land of the firebird: The beauty of old Russia,* New York: Simon and Schuster.
3. Gray, What is love?, 47.
4. Ibid., 48.
5. A. Toufexis (1993, February 15), The right chemistry: Biological and chemical factors in romantic love, *Time, 49* (3), 48–51.
6. D. Tennov (1979), *Love and limerence: The experience of being in love,* New York: Stein and Day.

CHAPTER 5

1. John 3:29, Revelation 18:23, 21:2, 9, and 21:17.

CHAPTER 7

1. J. T. Shawcross (Ed.) (1971), *The complete poetry of John Milton,* rev. ed., Garden City, NJ: Doubleday Anchor.
2. Speiser (1964) points out that the motifs of sexual awareness, wisdom, and nature's paradise that appear in the fall story are derived directly from *The Gilgamesh Epic.* Citing Pritchard in tablet 1, column iv, lines 16ff (*ANET,* p. 75), Enkidu is tempted by a courtesan, consequently repudiated by the world of nature, and acquires wisdom, which means a broader understanding. "Indeed the temptress goes on to tell him, 'You are wise Enkidu, you are like a god'; and she marks his new status by improvising some clothing for him" (column ii, lines 27f., *ANET,* p. 77). Speiser insists that the similarity between Genesis 3 and *The Gilgamesh Epic* is not mere coincidence. Moreover, the important issue is the fact that the

motifs of God withholding the benefits of both the tree of knowledge and the tree of life are borrowed from foreign sources, namely, *The Gilgamesh Epic* and the tale of Adapa (*ANET,* pp. 101ff).

3. An earlier exploration of this idea was presented in my Finch Lectures at Fuller Graduate School of Psychology in 1980 and subsequently published in J. H. Ellens (1982), *God's grace and human health,* Nashville, TN: Abingdon, chapter 3.

4. Jean Piaget, Lawrence Kohlberg, Erik Erikson, James Fowler, and Robert Fuller contributed significant works in the field of human personality development and maturation processes. Piaget focused upon cognitive development in children, Kohlberg on moral development, Erikson on social development, and Fowler on religious or spiritual development. These researchers constructed what may be called the Structuralist Model of human development. Robert Fuller analyzed the role of religious faith and worldview in the transitional steps from one stage of development to the next. He builds upon the work of the Structuralists and alludes to such other work as that of Don Browning, Carol Gilligan, Henry Maier, Robert Kegan, Gordon Allport, and others. These works are listed in the bibliography appended to this present volume. See also the work of Gail Sheehy and of Daniel Levinson.

5. H. Clinebell (1992), *Well being,* San Francisco: HarperSanFrancisco.

6. D. Capps (1990), *Reframing: A new method of pastoral care,* Minneapolis: Fortress.

CHAPTER 8

1. D. L. Ellens (1998), *A comparison of the conceptualization of women in the sex laws of Leviticus and in the sex laws of Deuteronomy,* Ann Arbor, MI: UMI.

2. Ibid. See J. A. Brundage (1987), *Law, sex, and Christian society in medieval Europe,* Chicago and London: University of Chicago Press, 1; and T. Frymer-Kensky (1992), Sex in the Bible, in her *In the wake of the goddesses,* New York: Fawcett Columbine, 197.

3. J. R. Wegner (1988), *Chattel or person?,* New York and Oxford: Oxford University Press, 11.

4. Ibid., 13.

5. M. Douglas (1966), *Purity and danger,* London: Routledge & Kegan, 53.

CHAPTER 9

1. D. L. Ellens (1998), *A comparison of the conceptualization of women in the sex laws of Leviticus and in the sex laws of Deuteronomy,* Ann Arbor, MI: UMI, 234–235.

2. Ibid., 251–252.

CHAPTER 10

1. B.W. Tuchman (1978), *A distant mirror: The calamitous 14th century,* New York: Knopf.

CHAPTER 11

1. Eventually in the life and practice of Israel it became standard practice to refer to the fact that perversion of the Yahwistic worship liturgies defiled the temple. That defiled the city and the people, as a result of which the defilement spread to the entire land of Israel. See the Prophecy of Ezekiel in which such generalized defilement is the framework of the story. Ezekiel is called, as a human being, to be priest and prophet, and to both measure the extent of the defilement and prepare for the purging of the evil from the liturgies of worship, from the temple, city, people, and land, so that God's domain could again be cleansed and rebuilt as the Kingdom of God.

2. A. Markels (2004), Love and Leviticus: Debating the Bible's stand on homosexuality, in *Mysteries of the Bible* (pp. 42–45), Washington, DC: U.S. News and World Report.

3. 2 Enoch, The Testament of the Twelve Patriarchs that includes the Testament of Benjamin and Naphtali, as well as the works of Josephus, are part of a body of literature written between 300 b.c.e. and 100 c.e., commenting on things having to do with the Hebrew Bible (OT) and related matters of Jewish history and culture up to the time of Christ, but they are not part of the Bible. They are instead part of what is these days called Literature of Second Temple Judaism. Some of that Second Temple literature is referred to as the Apocrypha and Pseudepigrapha.

CHAPTER 12

1. 2 Enoch, pp. 91–222 in J. H. Charlesworth (Ed.) (1983), *The Old Testament Pseudepigrapha,* Vol. 1, *Apocalyptic literature and Testaments,* Garden City, NY: Doubleday.

2. Ibid., 775–828

3. The Book of Jubilees, pp. 35–142 in J. H. Charlesworth (Ed.) (1985), *The Old Testament Pseudepigrapha,* Vol. 2, *Expansions of the "Old Testament" and legends, wisdom and philosophical literature, prayers, Psalms, and odes, fragments of lost Judeo-Hellenistic works,* Garden City, NY: Doubleday.

4. F. Josephus (1987), *The works of Josephus, complete and unabridged* (W. Whiston, Trans.), Peabody, MA: Hendrickson, 41.

5. See Brain feature linked to sexual orientation (1991, August 31), *Science News, 140,* 134; Genetic influence tied to male sexual orientation (1992, January 4), *Science News, 141,* 6; Genetic clue to male homosexuality emerges (1993, July 17), *Science News, 144,* 37; Homosexual parents: All in the family (1995, January 21), *Science News, 147,* 42; X chromosome again linked to sexuality (1995, November 4), *Science News, 148,* 295.

CHAPTER 13

1. See the *Encyclopaedia Britannica: Micropedia* (1974), Vol. 5, 15th ed., Chicago: William and Helen Benton, 323.

2. M.R. McMinn (1999), Dissociative Identity Disorder, in D.G. Benner and P.C. Hill (Eds.), *Baker encyclopedia of psychology and counseling*, 2nd ed., Grand Rapids, MI: Baker, 358; K.R. Krocke (1999), Anorexia Nervosa, in D.G. Benner and P.C. Hill (Eds.), *Baker encyclopedia of psychology and counseling*, 2nd ed., Grand Rapids, MI: Baker, 85.

3. G.L. Martin (1999), Child abuse, in D.G. Benner and P.C. Hill (Eds.), *Baker encyclopedia of psychology and counseling*, 2nd ed., Grand Rapids, MI: Baker, 179.

4. Ibid.

CHAPTER 14

1. J.B. Phillips (Trans.) (1958), *The New Testament in modern English*, London: Geoffrey Bles Ltd. and William Collins Sons & Co. Ltd., 343–344.

2. O. Piper (1960), *the biblical view of sex and marriage*, New York: Scribners, 19–21. See also O. Piper (1941), *The Christian interpretation of sex*, New York: Scribners.

3. D.E. Rosenau, J. Childerston, & C. Childerston (2004), *A celebration of sex after 50*, Nashville, TN: Nelson, 145.

BIBLIOGRAPHY

Aden, L., & J.H. Ellens (1990). *Turning points in pastoral care: The legacy of Anton Boisen and Seward Hiltner.* Grand Rapids, MI: Baker.

Allport, G. (1950). *the individual and his religion.* New York: Macmillan.

Bailey, D.S. (1955). *Homosexuality and the Western tradition.* London: Longmans.

Benner, D.G. (Ed.). (1985). *Baker encyclopedia of psychology.* Grand Rapids, MI: Baker.

Benner, D.G. & P.C. Hill (Eds.). (1999). *Baker encyclopedia of psychology and counselings,* 2nd ed. Grand Rapids, MI: Baker.

Brain feature linked to sexual orientation. (1991, August 31). *Science News, 140,* 134.

Browning, D. (1975). *Generative man.* New York: Delta.

Brundage, J. A. (1987). *Law, sex, and Christian society in medieval Europe.* Chicago and London: University of Chicago Press.

Capps, D. (1983). *Life cycle theory and pastoral care,* Philadelphia: Fortress.

Capps, D. (1990). *Reframing: A new method of pastoral care.* Minneapolis: Fortress.

Charlesworth, J.H. (Ed.). (1983). 2 Enoch. In *The Old Testament Pseudepigrapha,* Vol. 1, *Apocalyptic Literature and Testaments.* Garden City, NY: Doubleday.

Charlesworth, J.H. (Ed.). (1985). The Book of Jubilees. In *The Old Testament Pseudepigrapha,* Vol. 2, *Expansions of the "Old Testament" and Legends, Wisdom and Philosophical Literature, Prayers, Psalms, and Odes, Fragments of Lost Judeo-Hellenistic Works,* Garden City, NY: Doubleday.

Christian Reformed Church. (1973). *Acts of Synod.* Grand Rapids, MI: CRC Publications.

Clinebell, H. (1992). *Well being.* San Francisco: HarperSanFrancisco.

Cole, W. G. (1959). *Love and sex in the Bible.* New York: Association Press.

Douglas, M. (1966). *Purity and danger.* London: Routledge & Kegan.

Ellens, D. L. (1998). A comparison of the conceptualization of women in the sex laws of Leviticus and in the sex laws of Deuteronomy. Ann Arbor, MI: UMI. Rev. ed. forthcoming from London and New York: T&T Clark, a Continuum Imprint.

Ellens, J. H. (1982). *God's grace and human health.* Nashville, TN: Abingdon.

Encyclopaedia Britannica: Micropedia (1974). Vol. 5, 15th ed. Chicago: William and Helen Benton.

Erikson, E. (1962). *Young Man Luther.* New York: Norton.

Erikson, E. (1963). *Childhood and Society.* New York: Norton.

Erikson, E. (1964). *Insight and Responsibility.* New York: Norton.

Erikson, E. (1968). *Identity: Youth and Crisis.* New York: Norton.

Erikson, E. (1982). *The Life Cycle Completed.* New York: Norton.

Fowler, J. (1981). *Stages of faith: The psychology of human development and the quest for meaning.* New York: Harper & Row.

Frymer-Kensky, T. (1992). Sex in the Bible. In T. Frymer-Kensky, *In the wake of the goddesses.* New York: Fawcett Columbine.

Fuller, R. C. (1988). *Religion in the life cycle.* Philadelphia: Fortress.

Genetic clue to male homosexuality emerges. (1993, July 17). *Science News, 144,* 37.

Genetic influence tied to male sexual orientation. (1992, January4). *Science News, 141,* 6.

Gilligan, C. (1982). *In a different voice: Psychological theory and women's development.* Cambridge: Harvard University Press.

Gray, P. (1993, February 15).What is love? *Time,* 47–49.

Grundy, S. (2000). *Gilgames: A magnificent retelling of humankind's oldest epic adventure.* New York: HarperCollins/William Morrow.

Hiltner, S. (1972). *Theological dynamics.* Nashville, TN: Abingdon.

Hite, S. (1976). *The Hite report.* New York: Macmillan, London: Collier.

Homosexual parents: all in the family. (1995, January 21). *Science News, 147,* 42.

Hunter, R. J. (Ed.). (1990). *Dictionary of pastoral care and counseling.* Nashville, TN: Abingdon Press.

Jennings, T. W. (1990). Homosexuality. In R. J. Hunter (Ed.), *Dictionary of pastoral care and counseling* (529–532). Nashville, TN: Abingdon Press.

Josephus, F. (1987). *The works of Josephus, complete and unabridged* (W. Whiston, Trans.). Peabody, MA: Hendrickson.

Kegan, R. (1982). *The evolving self: Problem and process in human development.* Cambridge: Harvard University Press.

Keil, C. F., & Delitzsch, F. (1951). *The Pentateuch.* Vols. 1–3. Grand Rapids, MI: Eerdmans.

Kinsey, A. C. (1948). *Sexual behavior in the human male.* Philadelphia: Saunders; republished by Indiana University Press in 1998.

Kinsey, A.C. (1953). *Sexual behavior in the human female.* Philadelphia: Saunders; republished by Indiana University Press in 1998.

Kohlberg, L. (1981). *Essays in moral development.* Vol. 1 and 2, *The philosophy of moral development.* New York: Harper & Row.

Kosnik, A., et al. (1977). *Human sexuality.* New York: Paulist Press.

Krocke, K.R. (1999). Anorexia Nervosa. In D.G. Benner and P.C. Hill (Eds.), *Baker encyclopedia of psychology and counseling*, 2nd. ed., Grand Rapids, MI: Baker.

Levinson, D. (1978). *Seasons of a man's life.* New York: Knopf.

Maier, H. (1969). *Three Theories of child development.* New York: Harper & Row.

Markels, A. (2004). Love and Leviticus: Debating the Bible's stand on homosexuality. In *Mysteries of the Bible* (pp. 42–45). Washington, DC: U. S. News and World Report.

Martin, G.L. (1999). Child Abuse. In D. G. Benner and P. C. Hill (Eds.), *Baker encyclopedia of psychology and counseling,* 2nd. ed., Grand Rapids, MI: Baker.

Massie, S. (1980). *Land of the firebird: The beauty of old Russia.* New York: Simon and Schuster.

Masters, W.H. & Johnson, V.E. (1966), *Human sexual response.* Boston: Little and Brown.

McMinn, M.R. (1999). Dissociative Identity Disorder. In D.G. Benner and P.C. Hill (Eds.), *Baker encyclopedia of psychology and counseling*, 2nd. ed., Grand Rapids, MI: Baker.

McNeill, J. (1976). *The Church and the homosexual.* Kansas City: Sheed and Ward.

Miles, J. (1995). *God: A biography.* New York: Knopf.

Noth, M. (1965). *Leviticus: A commentary.* London: SCM Press.

Noth, M. (1967). *The laws of the Pentateuch.* Philadelphia: Fortress Press.

Olthuis, J. (1975). *I pledge you my troth.* New York: Harper.

Pattison, E.M. (1985). Homosexuality: Classification, etiology, and treatment. In D. G. Benner (Ed.), *Baker encyclopedia of psychology* (p.319–326). Grand Rapids, MI: Baker.

Phillips, A. (1961). *Ancient Israel's criminal law: A new approach to the Decalogue.* Oxford: Blackwell.

Phillips, J.B. (Trans.) (2000). *The New Testament in modern English.* London: Geoffrey Bles Ltd. and William Collins Sons & Co. Ltd.

Piaget, J. (1929). *The child's conception of the world.* London: Routledge & Kegan Paul.

Piaget, J. (1967). *Six psychological studies.* New York: Random House.

Piaget, J. (1970). *Structuralism.* New York: Basic Books.

Piper, O. (1941). *The Christian interpretation of sex.* New York: Scribners.

Piper, O. (1960). *The biblical view of sex and marriage.* New York: Scribners.

Pritchard, J.B. (1955). *Ancient Near Eastern texts relating to the Old Testament (ANET),* 2nd. ed., Princeton, NJ: Princeton University Press.

Rosenau, D.E., Childerston, J., & Childerston, C. (2004). *A celebration of sex after 50.* Nashville, TN: Nelson.

Schoeps, H.J. (1962). Homosexualität und Bibel. *Zeitschrift für evangelische Ethik, 6,* 371ff.

Shawcross, J.T. (Ed.) (1971). *The complete poetry of John Milton,* rev. ed. Garden City, NY: Doubleday Anchor.

Sheehy, G (1976). *Passages; Predictable crises of adult life.* New York: Dutton.

Simpson, C.A., & Bowie, W.R. (1952). The book of Genesis. In George A. Buttrick (Ed.), *The interpreters Bible,* Vol. 1. New York: Abingdon.

Snaith, H.N. (1967). *Leviticus and Numbers.* London: Nelson.

Speiser, E.A. (1964). Genesis. In W.F. Albright and D.N. Freedman (Eds.), *The Anchor Bible .* Garden City, NY: Doubleday.

Tennov, D. (1979). *Love and limerence: The experience of being in love.* New York: Stein and Day.

Toufexis, A. (1993, February 15). The right chemistry: Biological and chemical factors in romantic love. *Time, 49* (3), 48–51.

Tuchman, B.W. (1978). *A distant mirror: The calamitous 14th century.* New York: Knopf.

Von Rad, G. (1961). *Genesis: A commentary.* Philadelphia: Westminster Press.

Wegner, J.R. (1988). *Chattel or person?* New York and Oxford: Oxford University Press.

X chromosome again linked to sexuality. (1995, November 4). *Science News, 148,* 295.

INDEX

ABOUT THE SERIES EDITOR
AND ADVISORY BOARD

J. HAROLD ELLENS is a Research Scholar at the University of Michigan, Department of Near Eastern Studies. He is a retired Presbyterian theologian and ordained minister, a retired U.S. Army Colonel, and a retired Professor of Philosophy, Theology, and Psychology. He has authored, coauthored, and/or edited 72 books and 148 professional journal articles. He served 15 years as Executive Director of the Christian Association for Psychological Studies, and as Founding Editor and Editor-in-Chief of the *Journal of Psychology and Christianity.* He holds a Ph.D. from Wayne State University in the Psychology of Human Communication, a Ph.D. from the University of Michigan in Biblical and Near Eastern Studies, and master's degrees from Calvin Theological Seminary, Princeton Theological Seminary, and the University of Michigan. He was born in Michigan, grew up in a Dutch-German immigrant community, and determined at age seven to enter the Christian Ministry as a means to help his people with the great amount of suffering he perceived all around him. His life's work has focused on the interface of psychology and religion.

ARCHBISHOP DESMOND TUTU is best known for his contribution to the cause of racial justice in South Africa, a contribution for which he was recognized with the Nobel Peace Prize in 1984. Archbishop Tutu has been an ordained priest since 1960. Among his many accomplishments are being named the first black General Secretary of the South African Council of Churches and serving as Archbishop of Cape Town. Once a high school teacher in South Africa, he has also taught theology in college, and holds honorary degrees from universities including Harvard, Oxford, Columbia, and Kent State. He has been awarded the Order for Meritorious Service presented by President Nelson Mandela, the Archbishop of Canterbury's Award for outstanding service to the Anglican community, the Family of Man Gold Medal Award, and the Martin King Jr. Non-Violent Peace Award. The publications Archbishop Tutu has authored, co-authored, or made contributions to include No Future Without Forgiveness (2000), Crying in the Wilderness: (1986), and The Rainbow People of God: The Making of a Peaceful Revolution (1996).

LEROY H. ADEN is Professor Emeritus of Pastoral Theology at the Lutheran Theological Seminary in Philadelphia, PA. He taught full-time at the seminary from 1967 to 1994 and part time from 1994 to 2001. He served as Visiting Lecturer at Princeton Theological Seminary, Princeton, NJ on a regular basis. In 2002, he coauthored *Preaching God's Compassion: Comforting Those Who Suffer* with Robert G. Hughes. Previously, he edited four books in a Psychology and Christianity series with J. Harold Ellens and David G. Benner. He served on the Board of Directors of the Christian Association for Psychological Studies for six years.

DONALD CAPPS, Psychologist of Religion, is William Hart Felmeth Professor of Pastoral Theology at Princeton Theological Seminary. In 1989 he was awarded an honorary doctorate from the University of Uppsala, Sweden, in recognition of the importance of his publications. He served as president of the Society for the Scientific Study of Religion from 1990 to 1992. Among his many significant books are *Men, Religion and Melancholia: James, Otto, Jung and Erikson and Freud;* also *the Freudians on Religion: A Reader;* also *Social Phobia: Alleviating Anxiety in an Age of Self-Promotion;* and *Jesus: A Psychological Biography.* He also authored *The Child's Song: The Religious Abuse of Children.*

ZENON LOTUFO JR. is a Presbyterian minister (Independent Presbyterian Church of Brazil), a philosopher, and a psychotherapist, specialized in Transactional Analysis. He has lectured both to undergraduate and graduate courses in universities in São Paulo, Brazil. He coordinates the course of specialization in Pastoral Psychology of the Christian Psychologists and Psychiatrists Association. He is the author of the books, *Relações Humanas* [Human Relations]; *Disfunções no Comportamento Organizacional* [Dysfunctions in Organizational Behavior] and co-author of *O Potencial Humano* [Human Potential]. He has also authored numerous journal articles.

DIRK ODENDAAL is South African; he was born in what is now called the Province of the Eastern Cape. He spent much of his youth in the Transkei in the town of Umtata, where his parents were teachers at a seminary. He trained as a minister at the Stellenbosch Seminary for the Dutch Reformed Church and was ordained in 1983 in the Dutch Reformed Church in Southern Africa. He transferred to East London in 1988 to minister to members of the Uniting Reformed Church in Southern Africa in one of the huge suburbs for Xhosa-speaking people. He received his doctorate (D.Litt.) in 1992 at the University of Port Elizabeth in Semitic Languages. At present, he is enrolled in a Masters course in Counselling Psychology at Rhodes University.

WAYNE G. ROLLINS is Professor Emeritus of Biblical Studies at Assumption College, Worcester, Massachusetts, and Adjunct Professor of Scripture at Hartford Seminary, Hartford, Connecticut. His writings include *The Gospels: Portraits of Christ* (1964), *Jung and the Bible* (1983), and *Soul and Psyche, The Bible in Psychological Perspective* (1999). He received his Ph.D. in New Testament Studies from Yale University and is the founder and chairman (1990–2000) of the Society of Biblical Literature Section on Psychology and Biblical Studies.

ABOUT THE AUTHOR

J. HAROLD ELLENS is Editor for the Praeger Series in Psychology, Religion, and Spirituality. He is a Research Scholar at the University of Michigan Department of Near Eastern Studies, a retired Presbyterian theologian, an ordained minister, a retired U.S. Army Colonel, and a retired Professor of Philosophy, Theology, and Psychology. He served 15 years as Executive Director of the Christian Association for Psychological Studies, and was Founding Editor and Editor-in-Chief of the *Journal of Psychology and Christianity*. He has authored, coauthored, or edited 119 books, including *The Destructive Power of Religion*, 4 volumes (Praeger, 2004).

10/06